Missions, Evangelism, and Church Growth

Missions, Evangelism, and Church Growth

C. NORMAN KRAUS, Editor

HERALD PRESS
Scottdale, Pennsylvania
Kitchener, Ontario
1980

Library of Congress Cataloging in Publication Data

Main entry under title:

Missions, evangelism, and church growth.

"Given first as addresses in the Discipleship Lecture
Forum series sponsored by the Center for Discipleship
at Goshen College during the winter of 1979."
    Includes bibliographical references.
    1. Missions—Theory—Addresses, essays, lectures.
2. Mission of the Church—Addresses, essays, lectures.
3. Evangelistic work—Addresses, essays, lectures.
4. Church growth—Addresses, essays, lectures.
I. Kraus, Clyde Norman.
BV2063.M565   266   80-10922
ISBN 0-8361-1925-8

MISSIONS, EVANGELISM, AND CHURCH GROWTH
Copyright © 1980 by Herald Press, Scottdale, Pa. 15683
    Published simultaneously in Canada by Herald Press,
    Kitchener, Ont. N2G 4M5
Library of Congress Catalog Card Number: 80-10922
International Standard Book Number: 0-8361-1925-8
Printed in the United States of America
Design: Alice B. Shetler

15   14   13   12   11   10   9   8   7   6   5   4   3   2   1

Contents

Preface

The discussion of evangelism in the church at large is far livelier today than it has been for some decades. Both evangelicals and ecumenicals are reassessing its definition and place in the life of the church. The churches are searching for new directions in missions both for strategy and goals. We are clearly in a time of ferment.

Our essays investigate this varied and exciting scene. Some explain the history and theology that inform the new situation. Others evaluate some of the more recent ideas and theories about the goals of missions, and offer helpful findings and insights for those who are interested in building a dynamic growing congregation.

This is a symposium in which each essay is a complete presentation in itself. So one could begin reading anywhere one chooses. But the essays are complementary, and it may be particularly helpful to the uninitiated reader to first get the overview offered in the introduction.

The next two chapters on missions and salvation deal with the theology and history of the wider missionary endeavor of the church. Then follow essays on the responsibility and possible approaches of the congregation for a local witness. The chapter titles indicate the subjects treated. The last chapter presents both an evaluation of the Church Growth Movement from the perspective of the North American churches and the challenge which it urges upon us.

These chapters were given first as addresses on the Discipleship Lecture Forum series sponsored by the Center for Discipleship at Goshen College during the winter of 1979. The authors come from varied backgrounds, and no attempt was made to synchronize points of view. The purpose of the essays is to inform and stimulate discussion. Each author is responsible only for his own expressed opinions.

As editor I have exercised my prerogative to edit several of the addresses fairly extensively in order to make what were stimulating oral presentations also excellent written essays. I have tried, however, to retain completely intact the author's point of view, and to keep as much of his style as possible.

I sincerely hope that this symposium will commend itself to a wide reading audience, and will result in a more vigorous, authentic witness to Jesus Christ.

C. Norman Kraus
Center for Discipleship
1979

Missions,
Evangelism, and
Church Growth

1
Introduction: Evangelism, Missions, and Church Growth

C. NORMAN KRAUS

The relation of evangelism to mission and church growth is left wide open in the title of this book. Indeed, it was in some sense the task of each contributor to define that relationship. Is evangelism *the* mission of the church? Is the goal of that mission the numerical growth of the church? Some would relate the ideas in just that way: Evangelism is the mission, and church growth is the goal. Our symposium of essays raises questions about such a simplistic understanding. Is not the mission of the church more comprehensive than evangelism? What about the nurturing, fellowship, and social service aspects of mission? Are they not fundamental to the church's spiritual maturity and growth of influence? Does it help to simply redefine evangelization to include these other dimensions of the church's life and mission rather than to define it as a specific part of the church's witness?

And how shall we understand "growth"? Are we to make

C. **Norman Kraus** was until 1979 director of the Center for Discipleship and a professor at Goshen College, Goshen, Indiana. The author of several books, he is presently a missionary in Japan.

institutional growth the priority? With membership in the American churches decreasing and the population growth of the world far outstripping the numerical growth of the church it is understandable that there should be concern with numbers. But is the goal of the church simply to increase its size? What is the relation of quality and quantity of membership in church growth? And if we are concerned about quality of life and witness, what does that imply for the evangelization process? These questions are all spoken to in one way or another in these essays.

In this introductory chapter, I will address myself briefly to an overview of the subject. What are the new trends in evangelism? How has the church understood its missionary responsibility historically? And what new insights have come out of the discussions of the past decades? What is distinctive about the Church Growth Movement? And how has institutional growth been related to economic and cultural factors? (Miller, Bauman, and Wenger deal more specifically with those internal factors and characteristics that make for increase in congregational membership.)

Evangelism

In twentieth-century America evangelism and Evangelicalism had become increasingly identified. Revivalism and evangelism were virtually equated in the mass campaigns sponsored by cooperating denominations. The call for decisions in these meetings was jointly for reconsecration and initial acceptance of Jesus Christ. And it has been an axiom that effective evangelism is directly related to the revival of evangelical experience in the churches.

By and large these campaigns, which issued a general call and then provided for individual counseling, reached people who were already in the ambit of the churches. Indeed, some "evangelists" were quite explicit in claiming that the membership of the institutional church provided the most effective "fishing ground" for converts to Evangelical religion.

In addition to area wide campaigns, radio and television were used to reach a wider non-Christian audience. Tract ministries, rescue missions, personal visitations were also common methods of evangelism. And in all these cases evangelism was identified with the Evangelicals' passion to "win the lost," "save souls," lead people "to receive Jesus as Savior," or to be "born again." Mainline denominations, who were for the most part more liberal, shied away from such overt methods of evangelism and relied on traditional congregational activity such as worship and nurture, and on broad social witness to fill the ranks. Evangelism was broadly defined as Christian witness in congregational preaching, loving concern, and social service.

A Changing Situation

This conservative liberal difference of approach to evangelism continued to be a moot issue in the 1950s and early 1960s when there was a general and satisfying membership growth in most of the churches. Liberal analysts pointed out that very small percentages of those who made "decisions" in the mass campaigns actually found their way into the churches. Evangelicals countered that institutional church membership is not the criterion for true conversion. Decisions to receive Christ as Savior are. Then in the mid-60s it became apparent that the mainline denominations were beginning to have a serious erosion of membership. Not only did membership growth slow down, but there was an actual decline in total membership. This among other factors led to a renewed interest in evangelism.

Among conservatives the Church Growth Movement was beginning to have a major impact. Church Growth advocates challenged the assumption that the saved individual is the goal of evangelism. It refocused evangelical attention on the importance of gathering churches—cells of Christian fellowship.[1] Using this criterion the Church Growth analysts examined the results of traditional methods of evangelism and produced clear evidence that they were indeed inefficient in promoting *church* growth.[2] Still other evangelicals began to challenge the strict separation of evangelism and social service in the church's mission.[3]

All this has led to a vigorous discussion, redefinition and reassessment of the evangelistic ministry of the church. Careful studies have been made of what has actually brought people into the churches. More serious attention has been given to the communication process—the relation of words and deeds, use of "religious" terminology to relate the message, and the significance of culture as a vehicle of communication. New studies of the biblical meaning, methods, and goals of proclaiming the gospel have enlivened the debate.

Defining the Nature and Scope of Evangelism

While the definition of evangelism remains in dispute, there is broad concern to distinguish it from the more inclusive "mission" or "witness" of the church, and to give it its proper place among the various gifts of the Spirit to the church for the fulfillment of its mandate. Typical of this emphasis are the words of Wayne Schwab, evangelism and renewal minister of the Episcopal Church:

> Everything the church does is not evangelism. Evangelism is an identifiable, unique activity. It centers in the presentation of

Jesus Christ (encounter with him) and the response of faith (commitment to him and responsible membership in his Church). Liturgy, education, social ministry may have evangelistic elements but they are *not* evangelism. The Episcopal Church tends to mistake ministry to persons in need and work for social justice as evangelism. These must be done but they are not evangelism. We seem to have lost confidence in the power of the message to stand on its own. While it must always be lovingly presented, the Gospel does always go beyond whatever works of love and justice we do in its name.[4]

The new sensitivity to the way in which we actually communicate has led to emphasis upon the "relational" aspects of evangelism. Recent Inter-Varsity Fellowship literature on evangelism puts great stress on the importance of genuine friendship with and acceptance of sinners as they are.[5] Others stress the importance of integrity in sharing oneself. That means sharing weaknesses as well as strengths and pointing to Christ as the One who saves rather than to oneself as an example of salvation. One writer suggested that Christian evangelists should be "practiced listeners rather than habitual talkers." All stress the self-defeating effects of gimmickry. Recent studies show that marketing-oriented (selling) techniques have not won people to the church!

The relational aspect of communicating the gospel is pressed in yet another way. New stress is being placed on *lay* witness rather than professional preaching. In the Lay Witness Mission the free, unpretentious sharing of the story of Jesus and how it has affected the witness' own life was found to be highly effective. Evangelism is not only telling the story of Jesus, but relating that story to my own story and the story of the one to whom we are witnessing. As Louis Almen puts it, "The interrelationship of his [Jesus] story and my story provides the substance of my personal witness. How his story relates to the story of the person to whom we are witness ('your story') is crucial. Effective witnessing is telling Jesus' story in a way which is relevant to the listener."[6]

Finally, there is a new recognition of both the importance and the limitations of evangelism more narrowly defined. Evangelism was underemphasized in the Protestant Reformation, and it has seldom if ever been given priority in the typical congregations of mainline Protestant denominations. That is, it has generally been viewed as an individual and extra-congregational concern. Now the responsibility of the congregation to be an evangelistic witness in its life and message is being given a new and welcome emphasis. This is the burden of Howard Snyder in his *Community of the King*, and of his chapter in this book.[7] At the same time that we affirm this new emphasis on corporate witness we must also raise questions about the separation and possible lack of balance between evangelism and nurture in the writings of Church Growth advocates like Peter Wagner, Win Arn, and Donald McGavran. This "yes, but" is reflected in the essay by Harold Bauman which assesses the Church Growth Movement in chapter 7.

Mission and Missions

In the broadest sense the mission of the church is to proclaim the salvation of God in Christ to the world. In Ephesians Paul writes that God's plan for the ages has been finally revealed in Jesus Christ, and the church has been given the mandate to make this plan of salvation known to the world (3:9-10). This commission or mandate has been the basic motivation and justification for missionary activity or missions, and for many people *missions* (missionary activity or evangelism) are virtually synonymous with *mission*.

In this volume a distinction is made between the two. Mission is associated with God's mission in sending Christ to establish His rule and kingdom, and the implicit question to which our authors speak is what role the church plays in the fulfillment of God's mission. What are the implications of the mandate? And what strategy shall it follow to accomplish its task?

The answer to these questions will be determined largely by one's understanding of the meaning of salvation. If by salvation we understand simply "receiving Jesus as our personal Savior" from the spiritual consequences of sin, then evangelism or preaching the word of Christ's death and resurrection for our justification would seem to encompass the mission. But if we understand salvation to mean the coming of God's rule "on earth as it is in heaven" then the mission of the church includes broader social and political dimensions as well as evangelism.

Chapter three examines the meaning of salvation as it relates to mission and missions in the church. Here a brief historical overview of the concepts of salvation and missions will provide background for understanding the changes that have taken place in the concept of missionary activity.

Mission as Christianization

After the church became an established social institution in the fourth century it began to send missionary monks to the pagan countries north and east of the Roman Empire. From the beginning of this missionary activity these Roman Catholic missionaries who went into the wilds of central and northern Europe considered it their task to establish the institutional church and bring the population into it.

According to Roman theology, salvation could be found only in the Catholic Church because through it the sacraments are dispensed to individuals for their salvation. Baptism was the sacrament of regeneration which erased the flaw of original sin and freed the soul from its condemnation to hell. And the other sacraments, especially the Lord's Supper, were further "means of grace" through which salvation might be attained. Therefore the missionary sought first, by whatever means was available, to bring individuals to the baptismal fount.

In order for the church to be firmly established as an effective social institution the missionary needed political approval and sanction. Thus these missionaries usually worked to convince the rulers that Christianity was the true religion. When they accepted Christianity and the church as part of their sociopolitical identity, the realm was considered Christian. The conversion of the ruler assured that all those thereafter born within the realm would be baptized into the church. Once the convert had been sacramentally regenerated and identified with the church by baptism the task of civilizing and nurturing, that is, Christianizing, followed. This was a slow process that often took generations, and the final result was a "Christian civilization." The mission of the church was to create "Christian civilization."

Now, interestingly enough although the Protestant Reformers rejected the sacramental concept of salvation, they did not challenge the concept of Christianization. When in the seventeenth and early eighteenth centuries orthodox Protestants began to again evangelize those outside of Christendom, they conceived of the task as Christianization, but with a difference. They did not begin with baptism but with civilization.

Salvation was understood as justification and forgiveness of sin and its consequent punishment, and such justification was by faith alone, not by sacramental grace. By this time

Protestant theologians were interpreting faith as belief in orthodox theological doctrine. Thus the task of the missionary was first to civilize and teach. When the catechumens understood enough to make an orthodox confession of faith they could be baptized into the church.

In this Protestant Christendom model Christianity was identified with the "Christian civilizations" of Europe. So closely, for example, did the Puritans of New England identify Christianity and English Protestant culture that it seemed obvious to them that the "savage" Indians needed to first learn English civility before they could be evangelized. And once they were evangelized, they were settled in Christian villages where they could more easily follow at least a modicum of Puritan religious discipline. Salvation meant to be civilized after the model of Reformed Christianity and the mission of the church was to spread this civilization by Christianizing the pagan.

Mission as Evangelization

In the eighteenth century the Moravian Pietists introduced a variation of this concept of salvation which shifted the priority of the missionary task away from civilizing the "heathen." Count Zinzendorf held, as did most Protestant theologians, that strictly speaking individuals are saved by God's sovereign election. That is, they are chosen by God to be saved by the atoning death of Christ. But unlike most of the theologians of his day he held that God had elected individuals outside of Christendom, and that the Holy Spirit was already at work in their lives. Further, he said that the church has a mandate to preach Christ crucified as widely as possible so that the elect might hear and have their salvation "sealed." Thus the major emphasis was placed upon evangelism rather than Christianization.

One of these Moravians speaking about his missionary colleagues put it clearly in a journal entry in 1740:

> ... they determined in the literal sense of the word to preach Christ and him crucified, without laying first "the foundation of repentance from dead works, and faith towards God" [teaching preliminary theology and morals of Christian civilization]. ... This reached the hearts of the audience, and produced the most astonishing effects .... They remained no longer the stupid and brutish creatures that they had been .... A sure foundation being thus laid in the knowledge of a crucified Redeemer, our missionaries soon found that this supplied the young converts with a powerful motive to the abhorrence of sin and the performance of every moral duty towards God and their neighbor.[8]

Salvation meant to be moved by the Spirit of God to respond to the crucified Savior in penitence and devotion. The mission was to spread the message.

About a century later, from the 1830s following, the concept of salvation as a spiritual standing based upon election was strongly reasserted and spread by the Plymouth Brethren. The movement began in Ireland and Britain, but after the Civil War many in Canada and the United States also followed their teachings which were propagated in the Bible and Prophetic Conference movements. They conceived salvation as a heavenly and spiritual reality almost to the exclusion of its physical, psychological, and social dimensions. They held that the primary task of the church is evangelism, that is, the verbal proclamation of the Word. And they idealized the preacher with the open Bible as the symbol of the faithful church. Some even added that no one had a right to hear the message of the gospel twice until everyone had heard it once.

Although it was not entirely consistent with a theology of

election, they placed much stress upon the initial receiving of Christ into one's heart. This decision for Christ was equated with salvation, and they held that once individuals were saved they could not be eternally lost even though they might backslide. Relatively little emphasis was given to nurture and discipline. As long as there were souls to be saved the evangelistic task must have first priority.

Mission as "Building the Kingdom of God"

The Social Gospel movement of the early decades of this twentieth century offered still another concept of salvation, namely, as the culmination of the kingdom of God on earth. The kingdom of God was interpreted as the great ethical ideal for human society, and the mission of the church was to build the kingdom. Although the Social Gospel still maintained belief in individual salvation, it placed emphasis on "social redemption," and spoke of the kingdom as "humanity organized according to the will of God." Walter Rauschenbusch, one of its leading exponents, wrote of "Christianizing the social order" and of "the salvation of the superpersonal forces" by which he meant the economic, social, and political institutions of society.

Such concepts shifted missionary strategy from verbal evangelism to the evangelism of humanitarian service. Instead of converting individuals the aim was to change the social conditions which cause individuals to become enslaved to sin. While this movement did not issue in a distinctive missionary movement, it did have a pervasive influence on missionary motivation and strategy. For the first time service instead of conversion became the missionary motivation, and priority was given to building service institutions such as schools, hospitals, agricultural development, and the like.[9]

At the height of liberal influence in America a group of Christian laymen made a tour of missions in Asia, and in their report back to the American churches they added another dimension to this social definition of salvation. The kingdom of God, they said, is attained in "the full development of individuals, the maturing of social groups, and the spiritual unity of all men and races."[10] They envisioned a universal brotherhood of mankind which had arrived at spiritual truth and the meaning of life as God intends it.

The aim of missions, wrote William Ernest Hocking, the author of their report, is "to seek with people of other lands a true knowledge and love of God, expressing in life and word what we have learned through Jesus Christ, and endeavoring to give effect to his spirit in the life of the world."[11] And the method for missions is dialogue and common search with the leaders of other religious faiths. There should be no attempt to convert. Rather the ideal is for Christianity to permeate other, non-Christian cultures with the spirit of Jesus Christ.[12]

Mission as Proclamation and Service

When the liberal concept of the church's mission as an evolutionary spiritual dynamic in the world was enunciated by some delegates at the Jerusalem Missionary Conference (1928), it triggered an immediate strong protest from both conservative and neoorthodox Protestant missiologists. Conservative Protestants reaccentuated the definition of salvation as justification of the individual before God. They viewed it as a supernatural, spiritual transaction and insisted that the first priority of missions remains the verbal witness to Christ's atoning work. They reacted to what they considered a substitution of the social for the spiritual and of human effort for the supernatural work of God. If any social services such as education, health care, or child care were engaged in, they were justified as a means to preaching the gospel—as a kind of "pre-evangelism."

Neoorthodoxy also stressed the proclamation of the Word of God as a word of revelation uniquely different from the spiritual insights of great religious leaders. Thus they contended that there could be no "common search" for spiritual truths. The word of salvation is a revealed word. However, they gave more place to the church, rather than the individual, as the missionary agent and context for preaching. The church, they said, is the central instrument and sign of the kingdom of God in the world. The author of the now famous aphorism, "The church exists by mission as fire exists by burning," was H. E. Brunner, one of the movement's foremost theologians.

Thus neoorthodoxy took the church more seriously than did conservative Protestantism. The church in mission was itself part of the witness—a sign. Evangelization was more broadly defined as both proclamation and service. The proclamation was made in and through the church spreading throughout the world. The ministry of service and social concern was exercised through lay persons as their Christian calling, and was included as an integral part of the church's mission.

What we have been witnessing more recently in Evangelical mission circles, especially since the Lausanne Conference in 1974, is a growing proliferation of voices calling conservative Protestants to a more holistic view of mission which includes both word and deed, proclamation and social service, as integral parts of the witness to Jesus Christ. And from the side of the mainline Protestant denominations, sometimes referred to as the ecumenicals, we are seeing the same search for a new balance between deed and word. Indeed, one of the encouraging signs is that the ecumenical and evangelical theologians and mission strategists are beginning to dialogue again and are finding more common ground than either of them suspected was there. There is a common search for new directions in our changed and changing world. [13]

Church Growth

"In the latter years of the 1960s something remarkable happened in the United States: for the first time in the nation's history most of the major church groups stopped growing and began to shrink." So reported Dean Kelly in his book *Why Conservative Churches Are Growing* (1972). [14] The phenomenon that caught Kelly's attention was that some churches like the Seventh-Day Adventists, Jehovah's Witnesses, and Mormons were continuing to forge ahead while the mainline Protestant denominations were losing members. What made the difference?

Kelly noted that those groups which have clear, definite beliefs, who demand a high level of commitment from their members, who enforce their rules with discipline, and who have enthusiastic missionary zeal were growing. His book attempts to give the sociological explanation for this. Incidently, he uses the sixteenth-century Anabaptists as his first historical example of a "strong," growing religious group who demonstrated these characteristics.

Conversely he found that those groups which were characterized by relativism, diversity and tolerance, strong individualism, and reluctance to "impose" their own beliefs on others were precisely the ones that were not growing. Apparently also there was some correlation between the degree of relativism and ecumenical tolerance and the sagging membership statistics.

Kelly's work caused a flurry of excitement, and researchers set out to test his thesis. These studies indicated that socioeconomic and demographic factors apparently had more to do with a given local congregation's growth or decline than did Kelly's characteristics. Thus Carl Dudley reports, "As a comprehensive solution to the problems of membership growth and decline, the Kelly thesis is inadequate."[15]

Perhaps Kelly's thesis is too broad to apply to each specific congregational situation; and certainly it does not offer any guaranteed techniques for growth. Neither does it give sanction to every kind of conservative belief and church pattern so long as the religious group is growing. He did not make growth the final criterion of religious value. But his analysis clearly explores the relation of quality and quantity in the growth equation. What his data suggests at a minimum is that integrity of belief, strict group discipline, and demands for commitment (quality factors) can be positive rather than negative growth factors. Other studies since Kelly's have corroborated this thesis. And conversely, contrary to what might seem sociologically evident, compromise and tolerance which grow out of relativism and lack of precise convictions—those twin virtues of individualistic democracy—are not necessarily values in church growth.

Kelly's study offered a sociological analysis which attempted to account for the actual developments which he observed. Two other kinds of approach have been made to the study of church growth. The one inquires of those who have a satisfying church relationship what factors led them to choose their particular congregations. The other approach is to study the characteristics of growing congregations. Data from both of these types of research are interesting and significant.

A recent poll conducted by George Gallup for the Princeton Religion Research Center asked a carefully selected sample of the population why they chose the congregation in which they hold membership.[16] The highest percentage categories were as follows:

47% I was brought up in this congregation.
20% This church has good preaching.
18% I was invited by a member, and I liked the people.
18% This church had a good program of religious education for children and youth.
17% Close friends belonged to this church.
15% I found a pastor or church friends with whom I could openly discuss my spiritual needs.
11% I found a pastor or church friends with whom I could openly discuss my religious doubts.

Note that these last two are similar and involve a significant percentage of the respondents.

Other similar polls have disclosed much the same results. They seem to indicate that friendship and family ties are very important evangelistic factors. Warmth and openness of the congregation, and spiritual stimulation are also strong drawing cards. More formal programs of evangelism, crusades of one kind or another, and radio evangelism rate very low as factors which influence people to come into the church.

These findings are substantiated by studies of congregations that are in fact growing. Two of these studies that I have found instructive are the Southern Baptists' examination of the fifteen fastest growing congregations in their convention, and Edward Perry's findings in twenty-six Lutheran Church of America congregations in upper New York state.[17] Both of these simply tried to discover the significant characteristics of their growing churches, and they are in remarkable agreement in what they found.

First, a few random but significant factors: The Lutheran study emphasized that growth may reflect the retention of members who were potential "dropouts" and the reactivation of earlier members as well as new recruitment. This points to an important aspect of growth that is often overlooked. Growth depends not only on how many come into the church but how many stay in!

Second, both studies indicate that their growing churches are formed along culturally homogeneous lines. The Southern Baptists note that their typical fast growing congregation is white, middle class, family oriented, and in a white suburban neighborhood. And the Lutherans report that "people tend to join our congregations partially on the basis of their income, occupation, and social status." Both are uneasy about this observation and consider how it might be otherwise. "The church of Jesus Christ is not *supposed* to be that way," the Lutherans ruefully admit.

Third, both studies indicate that organized congregational campaigns and evangelistic programs were not particularly successful. And both in their own way note that running social service programs in the neighborhood does not seem to increase the congregational roll. Only when the pastor was closely involved visiting the people served did Lutheran congregations sponsoring social services experience growth.

Following are six characteristics of growing congregations which both reports seem to agree upon:

(1) Both observe that their growing congregations have strong, experienced pastoral leadership. The Baptists emphasize the pastor's vision, charismatic authority, and ability to mobilize the congregation behind his vision. The Lutherans observe a "benign authoritarian" style as the only pastoral factor that seemed to correlate with growth.

(2) Supportive, intimate relationships are an important factor. Perry lists it as of first importance. This factor includes both intracongregational relationships of nurture and support in times of need, and friendliness and acceptance of nonmembers. Baptists stress the effectiveness of *personal* visitation in evangelism. They were, however, leery of small groups. Both of these denominations are pastor-oriented and stress the role of the pastor in personal contact and counseling.

(3) The Bible is emphasized as an authority for life. Both mention sound biblically oriented preaching as an important ingredient in the successful congregation. Baptist preachers in the fastest growing churches tend to preach expository sermons, and talk about contemporary social issues only as they are mentioned or implied in the text.

(4) Both rely heavily on the quality of the Sunday morning worship experience. Satisfying, uplifting, enthusiastic worship both draws new members and retains the old ones.

(5) Growing congregations in both traditions reflect a positive missionary posture. Baptist pastors emphasize that evangelism must be made a priority goal of the congregation if growth is to occur.

(6) There is agreement, with some variation, on the need to train lay people thoroughly for the job of visitation and recruitment. The Lutherans noted that best results came when the pastor was personally involved, and laity need to be both carefully selected and prepared if they are to be used. Baptists are more team oriented and provide a variety of training programs.

It should be noted that these observations do not describe techniques or principles that are guaranteed to work in every situation. All, including the Church Growth advocates who claim that the study of church growth can be made into a science, agree that the external social, economic, and demographic conditions differ so much from congregation to congregation that no one set of principles or techniques can be enunciated for all. And all agree that it is the Holy Spirit who gives healthy growth to the body of Christ. From the human side we need to use much spiritual creativity and practical ingenuity in the application of these data to our own congregations.

Conclusion

We began this introductory chapter by raising the question of the relationship between evangelism, mission, and church growth. In closing now we return to this same question and view it from a New Testament perspective. The New Testament itself is the product of a great burst of missionary activity. It reflects the initial founding and the rapid expansion of the church, and as such it is a significant source of data on church growth and mission.

The New Testament suggests a different paradigm or relational pattern of evangelism, mission, and growth than that offered in many contemporary Evangelical discussions. Instead of identifying evangelism with the mission and growth as the goal of the mission, the New Testament writers speak of growth as a basic prerequisite for accomplishing the mission, and evangelism as one means of achieving its goals. The goals of mission are neither church growth nor the preaching of the gospel. But this reorients the meanings of these words. This statement needs further explanation.

The apostles, that is, those to whom the mission was first assigned, and especially Paul who was the greatest missionary evangelist of all times, were obviously engaged in the extension of the church through the multiplication of

Christian congregations. That is not in dispute. Further, they addressed themselves to the task of winning new converts to the cause of Christ. Paul's consuming passion was to save as many as possible by all means possible. But his *mission* was not simply to reach the greatest possible number of souls and form them into Christian fellowships. His mission was to bring the whole world into subjection to Jesus Christ as Lord so that it might be saved.

Two distinguishable aspects are implied in this cosmic mission committed to the church. First, the "whole world" means all peoples of the earth. The mission is to bring all peoples of the earth under the lordship of Christ, that is, make them disciples. Second, included in the "whole world" are the "principalities and powers"; and Paul understands that the church's mission includes making known to these authorities the true nature of God's plan of salvation.

The ringing affirmation of Paul's gospel is that Jesus, the risen Messiah, is indeed Lord. He has disclosed the meaning of creation and the fulfillment of history—both our personal histories and the world's history. Salvation is to be found through submission to His authority (repentance) and following His commandment (love). This same emphasis is found in Matthew 28:19-20. To make all people *disciples* is to bring them into subjection, that is, under the tutelage of Christ as Master. They are to be pledged to a new loyalty (baptizing) and carefully trained to follow the new pattern of relationships exemplified and commanded by Christ (teaching).

Growth in the New Testament is most often used to indicate development toward maturity in the body of Christ (e.g., Ephesians 4:13-16). But it can also be applied to the increase of the number of disciples and the multiplication of churches (Acts 2:47). Growth in both of these senses is important for the effective execution of the mission which has been given to the church. Obviously, if there is no expansion of the number of subjects, the rule of God will be circumscribed. And equally where the loyalty, understanding, and character of the subjects are in question this rule will be impeded. The goal of the mission, however, is not greater numbers of disciples but the defeat of all the powers, human and superhuman, which do not serve the will of God. Growth, especially numerical growth, is a penultimate end, what John Dewey called a "means-end." This distinction, although it seems subtle is, nevertheless, extremely significant. It is a matter of placing first things first—the kingdom of God and not the church which is only an instrument of God in establishing His rule.

Finally, the method which Jesus taught for accomplishing the mission is the *proclamation* of the gospel both in word (evangelism) and in demonstration of the new reality which has been brought into effect by it. In his great concern to promulgate the message of the gospel Paul urges those who have joined him in the task to "walk worthy" of that message as living examples of its power and authenticity.

Gerhard Friedrich points out that this dual meaning of pronouncement and demonstration are implicit in the New Testament word for evangelize (*euangelidzesthai*).

Euangelidzesthai is not just speaking and preaching; it is proclamation with full authority and power. Signs and wonders accompany the evangelical message. They belong together, for the Word is powerful and effective. The proclamation of the age of grace, of the rule of God, creates a healthy state in every respect. Bodily disorders are healed and man's relation to God is set right. Joy reigns where this Word is proclaimed. It brings salvation .... The Holy Spirit ... attests Himself now in the time of fulfilment when the glad tidings are proclaimed. ...[18]

Perhaps what we need today in the church is less technique and more genuine proclamation in authentic word and deed. Indeed, even our polls and other empirical research seem to be telling us that.

2
The Changing Role of the Missionary: From "Civilization" to Contextualization

WILBERT R. SHENK

Each generation lives with the illusion that it has made a great discovery: the world is changing because of new forces and new opportunities; the world is not as it used to be. In leafing through the missionary literature of the past sixty years, I have been struck with how frequently writers of the past two generations have been preoccupied with the theme of missions having come to "the end of an era." Yet in 1978 a British missionary leader, Elliott Kendall, published a new book entitled *The End of an Era—Africa and the Missionary* (SPCK).

Before we dismiss the matter as self-evident, however, let us make two observations. First, the kind of change we are discussing is not the change measured by the number of new gadgets on retail counters or the never-ending appearance of new models of Fords and Chevrolets. Technological

Wilbert R. Shenk of Elkhart, Indiana, is secretary of overseas missions for Mennonite Board of Missions. He is editor of the mission journal *Mission-Focus*.

developments and the fads of fashion contribute to and reflect elements of change, but we are speaking about far more profound and far-reaching shifts in cultural values and world-view. Second, such basic change does not come quickly. It occurs over a period of a generation or more and consists of a multitude of small changes which come to focus in a major event such as a war or political upheaval. In a word, the role of the missionary has been changing for a long time.

Philosophers, historians, and sociologists have concentrated much energy on examining what happens to a civilization as it moves from one period to another. Rapid transition brings trauma and disintegration. Old values appear obsolete to many people, and they reach for new but untried alternatives. Other people recoil and attempt to reinforce the traditions against encroaching modernity. People's moods oscillate between despair and optimism. Many people revel in being able to rid themselves of what they consider a burdensome past, but they lack a credo by which to live the future. Thus, "the end of an era" is more than a pat phrase. It points to a particular moment in history when profound change occurs and we move from one order to another—a change in ethos, in values, in myths, in political relationships, in economic systems.

Our task in this chapter is to examine this "changing role." We want to trace the shift in missionary outlook from the time when all missionary action proceeded from the assumption that the first job was to "civilize" people in order that they might become Christians, to the present day when brothers and sisters in the Third World are challenging us to "contextualize" our efforts. We are being called to move from methods which produced dependence on us to an approach based on interdependence in relationship. We will pursue our theme by studying five key elements in missionary action, noting past practices and assumptions and what seems to be emerging for the future.

The Changing Concept of Mission

Our concept of the missionary task is conditioned by our perceptions, understandings, and assumptions about our world. We make certain assumptions about what the gospel is and how it is to be transmitted. We have certain understandings about the nature of the church in relation to mission. We have perceptions of God's purposes in and for the world and of how mission relates to those purposes. We make evaluations of human culture—positive or negative. Roman Catholics, for example, have traditionally taken a more positive attitude toward culture than have Protestants. This attitude led them to demand less of a break between culture and religion than Protestants demanded of converts in the missionary situation. And among Protestants substantial variations exist. For our purposes here we want to examine a broadly representative concept, laying aside shades of difference and exceptions to the general pattern.

The seventeenth-century New England Puritan missionaries largely set the course for modern missions. They defined their task as preaching the gospel so that Native Americans would be converted and receive personal salvation. But early in their missionary experience these New Englanders concluded that Indian converts could only be Christians if they were "civilized." The model by which they measured their converts was English Puritan civilization. These missionaries felt compassion and responsibility for their converts. They gathered these new Christians into churches for nurture and discipline and set up programs to transform Christian Indians into English Puritans.

From this emerged the slogan, "Civilization and Christianity," which was shorthand for saying that native peoples and their cultures had to be made over in the likeness of European culture. They assumed that European culture was synonymous with Christian culture. Therefore, to be a Christian required that the convert adopt European culture. All other cultures were "heathen" and depraved. Christianization was the same as civilization.

From time to time a few Protestant voices dissented from this prevailing concept. The Moravians in the eighteenth century adopted a strategy of migration and self-support which caused them to view much more sympathetically the cultures into which they moved. Missionaries often felt deep disgust and chagrin at the bad moral example set by fellow Europeans who traveled the length and breadth of the world as explorers, sailors, traders, and rulers and could hardly be called exemplary Christians. Nevertheless, no one doubted the inherent superiority of "Christian" European culture, and most viewed it as the necessary context for the Christian life.

In the nineteenth century a third "C," namely *commerce* emerged in the strategy for Protestant missions. Missionaries joined politicians and humanitarians in vigorous efforts to eradicate slavery. In time they concluded that the only lasting solution to slavery was to introduce legitimate trade which would make slave-trading economically unattractive. Thus, *commerce* joined *civilization* and *Christianity* to form the threefold flag under which the missionary ship sailed for the next two generations.

The prevailing concept of mission during the past three centuries was based on the inherent superiority of Western "Christian" culture and the inferiority and depravity of all other cultures. This condescension runs through the large three-volume study by James S. Dennis, *Christian Missions and Social Progress* published between 1897 and 1908. Dennis wrote:

> Nothing can be more interesting and touching to a sympathetic student of human progress than the phenomena which accompany the awakening of races just emerging from barbarism to the consciousness of the larger knowledge, the nobler morality, and the higher destiny which Christian civilization offers. It is like God's voice saying after long ages of darkness, "Let there be light." It is the sign of a new creative era in social history, in contradistinction to the long, uneventful periods of primitive savagery.[1]

The withering effects of this attitude survive to this day. In some non-Western people it produced a prideful rejection of things Western and Christian. In others it destroyed their own self-esteem. Many Native Americans of North and South America embody the results of a long campaign which told them their culture was worthless and they were subhuman. To counteract this attitude Albert Buckwalter, a Mennonite missionary, has spent twenty-five years translating the Bible into the Toba language to help the Toba people know that God speaks to them in their own language and that their culture is precious in the sight of their Creator.

This uncritical confidence in so-called Christian culture and equally uncritical rejection of other cultures blinded missionaries to the need to be critical of *all* cultures. At the same time it slowed the process of finding the positive values and points of reference in a given culture to which Christian faith could relate and on which the church could build.

After generations of missionary work, a few thoughtful observers in the nineteenth century began to detect the fallacies in these assumptions and to call for change. First, they rejected the emphasis on "civilizing" people, that is, imposing Western civilization upon them, as preparation for Christianizing them. Although the discipline of anthropology was not yet born, missionaries had done a considerable amount of spadework through their observation of other cultures and a close study of languages. They identified elements in these cultures which had positive value and which might prepare for the coming of the gospel. Second, by 1850 missionary leaders began to call for the *indigenization* of the church, that is, to adapt the Western forms and message to the culture in which it was transplanted. They noted that churches which had existed for a generation or longer were not thriving because they depended on the mission for sustenance. They emphasized the need for the church to become self-sufficient in leadership, financial support, and in evangelization. Although this represented a step forward, indigenization still assumed that the local church had to accept the Western model. Missions have continued to wrestle with this problem well into the present century.

Future Directions

What should our direction for the future be? Actually the answer to this question has been given repeatedly over a long period of time. Wherever missions have gone, local Christian movements have emerged which were independent of the mission and which saw themselves as providing a corrective to mistakes the missionaries made. One thinks, for example, of the *"No Church"* movement in Japan, the *Little Flock of Jesus* and related movements in China, the *Bahkt Singh* movement in India, and the extensive independent church movement throughout the African continent. Each of these movements affirmed and accepted the Christian gospel as their own, but at the same time protested against the way they felt Western Christians had failed to appreciate them and their own culture. They wanted to be taken seriously in their own cultural context. They fretted over the missionary version of the gospel which smacked too much of Western culture to be palatable to an Asian, a Latin American, or an African. For the gospel to be credible in the future, it must be allowed to do its work in each particular cultural context.

The nature of the problem caused by the traditional approach of transplanting Western models and the direction of future strategies is clearly illustrated in the manner theological education has been done on the mission fields. Hugo Zorrilla notes that theological education in Latin America is in a crisis today as a result of past patterns and he gives four specific reasons. First, theological education in Latin America is dependent upon an imported theology—a theology which can readily be traced to Europe or North America. Second, it is in crisis because it is merely copying curricula developed for other parts of the world. Third, Latin American theological schools suffer from a dearth of textbooks written by Latin Americans for use in Latin America. Finally, most theological schools in Latin America are staffed by teachers from North America and Europe.

If one adds to these criticisms, which are not peculiar to Latin America, the fact that these training programs are based upon a Western professional model of the ministry which assumes that a pastor will be fully supported by the congregation, it becomes obvious that such programs are ill-suited to the needs of the churches in many cultures.

No wonder leaders of churches in other parts of the world are calling for training programs which take seriously indigenous leadership patterns, including methods of financial

support. Few churches in these other continents have sufficient funds to be able to provide full financial support to
their pastors. Furthermore, it remains to be proved that the
Western professional model is really consistent with the biblical standard.

These leaders want to see leadership training programs
emerge which take into account educational methods indigenous to their cultures. For example, the time-honored
educational method in India was for a teacher to gather
round him disciple-learners who lived close to the master
teacher, listened to his wisdom, and observed him as he
ministered. This is of course the same pattern Jesus used
with His disciples.

Jonathan Chao, dean of the China Graduate School of
Theology, Hong Kong, has spoken to this issue:

> Traditionally, theology taught in the West is dogmatic,
> centered around creeds, and systematic, logically arranged, but
> influenced by historical controversies and molded by the philo-
> sophical thinking of its era (e.g., rationalism). We as Chinese
> cannot do anything about that, but do not want our schools
> dominated by that.[2]

Chao wants his people to be free to invest their energies in
studying biblical theology as the history of salvation. He
insists that it is important for the Chinese church to focus on
the problems confronting China in the 1980s rather than
sixteenth-century Europe or the America of the 1920s. Chao,
therefore, calls for a "theological liberation movement" and
even a "moratorium" on Western theological educators in
Asia. What he longs for is an "indigenous theology"
developed by Chinese, in Chinese language, and geared to
the Chinese church. To achieve his goal Chao advocates
what he calls the "man-and-task-oriented approach" instead

of a Western curriculum. This approach consists of three parts: communal life, academic program, and supervised practice. He wants to emphasize the importance of developing the students' spiritual life.

This concern for a missionary approach which starts with the cultural context of those to whom the missionary message is addressed is shared by people all across the theological spectrum. The ecumencially sponsored Theological Education Fund pioneered in studies that produced several influential reports. The same concern also emerged among evangelicals who are working at models for theological education by extension.

Changing Assessment of Culture

This decisive shift in concept to an emphasis on context came about gradually and as the result of a wide range of forces. The growing authority of the social sciences was one of these influences. A little journal called *Practical Anthropology,* of which a total of nineteen volumes appeared (1953-72), played a decisive role. Founded and edited by Eugene Nida and colleagues who enjoyed full standing within professional circles as well as wide acceptance among missionaries, *Practical Anthropology* helped mediate basic insights from linguistics and anthropology to the missionary in the field.

Missionaries based their changed attitude toward "non-Christian" cultures on the premise that every culture can be the vehicle through which Christian faith is transmitted and in which God's people can live. In contrast to earlier generations, social scientists have forced us to take a new look at culture. The old notion about a culture being "primitive" has undergone revision. We have discovered, for instance, that many other peoples of the world consider Western culture to be crude and unsophisticated. At the same time the West has come to recognize the sophistication, in terms of human relationships and social system, of many cultures once considered "primitive." A close study of the languages of so-called primitive peoples has revealed an amazing complexity in structure and nuance. Whereas Western people tend to measure culture development in terms of technological advance, other cultures emphasize the maintenance of proper human relationships.

All of this leads us to recognize that no culture can stand in judgment over other cultures. All cultures are relative before God. Furthermore, the gospel addresses every people in their own culture, bringing profound crisis and calling for decision. People do not need to step outside of their own milieu in order to respond to the gospel. We recognize that the Holy Spirit is active among all peoples, and, indeed, precedes the missionary who goes to witness among a people.

This deepening respect for culture as the context for all human life enables us to respect more fully each human being. Every person is a product of a culture and cannot be separated from that cultural heritage. The gospel itself respects this fact and speaks to the individual *in context*. We violate people when we try to force them to step outside their culture in order to be Christians.

In this connection, it is good to remind ourselves of the meaning of the recent emergence of ethnic consciousness. This development is not restricted to blacks or Native Americans. It is a worldwide phenomenon representing one of the most powerful forces in today's world. In our own society the rise of ethnic consciousness has exploded the old myth that America is a "melting pot." Social scientists tell us that ethnic conflict is the major source of violence in all countries and, in some cases, is leading to international conflict as well. This observation should cause us to reflect on the meaning of this consciousness and whether it is in fact a positive force.

Message and Paramessage

We are accustomed to speak about the missionary message as a key element in missionary self-understanding. I have deliberately chosen to use the term "paramessage" because it can help us identify an aspect that we dare not miss. The prefix "para" refers to that which covers or shields. Parasol, for example, describes an apparatus which shields one from the sun. By paramessage, then, we are referring to those cultural, national, and denominational factors that shield or filter the intended message of the gospel.

The missionary message as preached and taught over the past several centuries has remained fairly constant and consistent. But the audiences listening to and observing this message in widely different contexts often picked up quite different meanings. In his study of the church in Buganda, John V. Taylor noted that the missionaries had consistently preached a message which emphasized "the sinful condition of man, the atonement and the saviorhood of Christ, the conversion of the individual through conscious repentance and faith, and the offer of sanctification through the Holy Spirit conditioned by the surrender of the believer's will." What came through to the Buganda people, however, was primarily a word about the transcendent God.

"Katonda," the unknown and scarcely heeded Creator, was proclaimed as the focus of all life, who yet lay beyond and above the closed unity of all existence. This in itself was so catastrophic a concept that, for the majority of hearers, it appeared to be the sum of a new teaching. It was as though the missionaries preached Paul's gospel to Corinth, but their converts heard Paul's sermon to the Athenians mingled with Isaiah's message to the city of Jerusalem.[3]

The problem of communication consists of several levels. On the first level we face the basic challenge of translation from one language to another. Anyone who studies another language soon is up against the challenge of finding the word which is the precise equivalent of a particular term in the mother tongue. The second level takes us a step farther. It is not enough to simply translate words; one must find equivalent concepts. What do you do if the language which you are learning lacks words to describe the concept of sin or salvation or the future life? In some languages there are many terms for particular deities, but no comprehensive term for God as found in the Bible.

At the third and most fundamental level one must come to grips with the question of the world-view which informs a particular culture. What is the central dynamic at work among a people? Protestant theology has emphasized the problem of personal guilt and the need for cleansing from sin following Martin Luther's experience and teaching of justification by faith. However, the majority of the world's cultures know little, if anything, about the problem of guilt. They are preoccupied, as is the Bible, with shame. The peoples in many cultures have a vivid sense of the presence of evil powers and live in dread of these powers. A sensitive witness must take this reality seriously.

To the problem of language and world-view we must now add the paramessage. Here we refer to aspects of the missionaries' personalities or cultural baggage which get between them and their audiences. A missionary's cultural makeup creates one such paramessage. The people in Accra have no difficulty in describing a particular missionary's hymnody as "so American." To the people in Jakarta a certain missionary's manner is "typically English." This may sound fairly harmless; but if the hearers perceive that to the missionary these cultural values and folkways are hightly important and are, in fact, intermingled with the Christian message, they become either confused or resentful of this ethnocentrism.

Another paramessage may emerge out of a missionary's national background. The "ugly American" syndrome refers not simply to cultural insensitivity but to the deep-seated fear and resentment many peoples of the world have toward the United States' political and economic domination during the past generation. Colonialism still lives in the memory of many peoples and they do not welcome the prospect of a new colonial master. Missionaries cannot totally disengage themselves from their nationality, but those who fail to see how national background may becloud the Christian message they seek to share invite confusion and mistrust. They must be willing to dissociate themselves from political and economic designs which run counter to the gospel.

A third paramessage stems from denominationalism. Non-Western Christians have sharply criticized missions for the way in which they have exported denominational divisions and the spirit of divisiveness. The denominational additive can easily take precedence over the biblical witness. In the process the missionary's audience is denied a clear presentation of the gospel.

What is the alternative to these paramessages? Although we may well recognize the problems others have created, we must humbly accept the fact that each of us will create our own unique set of paramessages in the future. While we cannot eliminate the paramessages entirely, we can orient our ministry around certain understandings that will help to correct and even dissolve some potential misunderstandings.

In the first place, the missionary's message must always have about it a *universal* ring. It is addressed to all peoples and is not limited racially or geographically. On the basis of biblical authority we are able to affirm the value of each people and their culture. That is not to say that everything in a given culture is right or acceptable in the eyes of God. But we can begin with basic affirmation. We can acknowledge the positive values of each people's history while at the same time recognizing that all human cultures stand under God's judgment. It is not for the missionary to act as the judge but to bear witness to the One who will judge with righteousness, mercy, and truth. The missionary's message is a universal one because it alone calls the peoples of the world to make God their King, and to become a part of His people. This call is not to deny their culture or their ethnic history, but rather to find its fullness within God's purposes. If we understand the gospel in this universal framework, then we can address in a new way the problems of race, war, economic greed, and selfishness which divide the peoples of the world. The context for Christian ethics must be this universal peoplehood rather than national, ethnic, or tribal considerations.

We must also insist on keeping the missionary witness *biblical*. God's word written provides a common starting point for understanding the good news about Jesus Christ regardless of the language we use. Furthermore, to be biblical is to recognize that the message is rooted in God's love and His purposes for all the world.

While the missionary message is universal, it must also be concrete and specific in the sense that it addresses each particular individual in his or her context. It must not come as news intended to reach someone else in another time or place. The witness must speak to individuals in their condition and need.

This tension between the universal and particular elements in the gospel is a real one. In the past emphasis has been placed on the universal unchanging message. Today the change is toward the preaching of a message adapted to the concrete situation, and this raises for some the spector of "syncretism," that is, compromising the message by adapting it too uncritically to the local culture.

In the traditional view "syncretism arises in the course of presenting Jesus Christ as sole Lord and Savior to people of other religions living in cultures not molded in the biblical revelation. By translating the gospel into local languages, adapting or accommodating to local ideas and customs, these are absorbed into the life of the church."[4] In the future, however, we can expect the concern for syncretism to be redirected. Already some leaders of non-Western churches are expressing concern over the way in which the church in Europe and North America is trapped in corrupted versions of Christian faith. They are pointing out to us that Western Christianity is an amalgam consisting of some gospel along with a good deal of Western culture. Thus it also represents a compromised, impure, or syncretistic version of the Christian faith.

The New Relation of Church and Mission

The course of modern missionary history, theologically speaking, followed the path of mainline Protestantism. When the major sixteenth-century Protestant Reformers rejected the authority of Matthew 28:19-20 for contemporary Christians, they made it impossible for the church to view itself as existing for mission. Lone individuals within the

Protestant mainstream dissented from the prevailing view, but official censure and opposition blunted their influence. One thinks, for example, of the nobleman Justinian Welz (1621-1668?) who published three books passionately appealing to fellow Christians to launch out in world mission. Failing to arouse church leaders to their missionary responsibility, Welz took matters into his own hands and went as a missionary to Surinam where he died shortly after his arrival.

The Pietist movement provided the main impetus for European missions to non-Western cultures. Individuals or small groups of committed people, inspired by their new religious experience, organized missionary-sending societies, but their example failed to capture the imagination and commitment of Protestant church leaders. Because the church hierarchy refused to support and promote missions, the church did not throw its weight behind missionary action. Understandably mission supporters, acting on the basis of private interest and support, felt little need for the church. This resulted in a church without mission and mission without church.

Evangelicals reinforced this pattern with their heavy emphasis on the doctrine of individual salvation. The evangelical tradition has acted as though personal salvation is experienced apart from a commitment to the church, and this has affected evangelical patterns in various areas. The creation of independent missionary societies has maintained this chasm between church and mission rather than bridging it. The result has been a theology of evangelism and mission to which the church was extraneous.

Fortunately here and there in evangelical circles as well as in the broader missiological community, this view is changing. Writers like Howard Snyder (*The Community of the*

King, InterVarsity, 1978) are calling evangelicals to develop a doctrine of the church. We must come to see that mission is constituent to church. From a biblical point of view the one does not exist apart from the other. The church is essential to mission because it is the major instrument God uses in introducing His reign on earth. The church is intimately bound to mission because its life portrays before the world what the gospel means and is to do for the world.

In order to clarify our understanding of the nature and mission of the church, we need to consider the missionary implications of the marks of the church. The first mark of the church is *witness.* Continued witness to the Word serves not only to sustain the community of faith, it also is the means by which other people are introduced to the faith and led to commitment to the lordship of Christ. The church is comprised of people who have responded to good news about Jesus Christ and who are now orienting their lives around His will for them. Thus they have not only made an initial response to this good news but continue to listen to the proclamation of His Word to sustain and nourish their commitment to Him. But proclaiming and demonstrating the Word is never a purely parochial affair. Through witness the community of faith is established for the purpose of extending that witness to the world in order "that the world might believe." Witness is a dynamic movement outward and inward.

In the second place the church is marked by *fellowship.* The church consists of individuals who have been reconciled to God and one another. It is called into being by an act of the Holy Spirit, and it is experienced as the "fellowship of the Holy Spirit." This fellowship is the context for each member to experience love and forgiveness, to be nurtured, to grow, and to live out their salvation.

The fellowship of the Spirit is a center for redemptive action. The Holy Spirit endows the people of God with spiritual gifts, and among these gifts are those by which they reach out to the world in witness and service. The variety of witness and service gifts are discerned and exercised through this fellowship which is not closed to the world but is specially equipped for ministry to the world.

The third mark of the church is *service*. Jesus modeled the servant role for us. In so doing He not only depicted the stance the church is to assume toward the world but revealed the peculiar motivation which enables the church to respond to the world in this way. The "upside-downness" of the kingdom of God is most clearly reflected in the way it handles power in relation to the world. Servanthood is the way God's people employ the power of the kingdom. The novelty of Christian service emerges at this point. As the church moves among the peoples of the world, it does so as the body of Christ in the spirit of Christ. The church is sent out as a servant of the King who is establishing His reign among people on the basis of love and justice.

Following the suggestion of the Dutch mission scholar Johannes Verkuyl, we note a fourth mark of the church, the *struggle for justice*. The church is caught up in a struggle for justice because God's righteousness is expressed in justice. God's new creation represents this new order of salvation where justice is a reality. The church enters a struggle for justice first of all by ordering its own life along these new lines. Beyond that, however, the church takes seriously the hurts, pains, failures, and frustrations of the oppressed of the world, on the one hand, and the people and powers who oppress them, on the other. The church is called to demonstrate God's new order and then to prophesy to the world against sin and oppression and announce God's coming reign of justice/righteousness.

The changing perception of the relation of church and mission is challenging the role of the missionary. Local believers cannot understand a missionary who refuses to identify as a member of the local fellowship or who acts as though a missionary cannot receive pastoral care and learn spiritual lessons from the local body. The church wants the missionary to be one of its links with the worldwide body, an intermediary who helps the local church find its role as a part of the larger body of Christ.

Method: From Institution to Relationship

Missionary method during the past 200 years has been tied to the concept of institution. The term "institution" does not point to specific institutional forms such as hospitals or schools, but rather to a basic mind-set and the methodology it produced. For example, institution suggests *permanence*. Words such as "compound" and "mission station" indicate a permanent physical layout. We speak also of a "compound mentality" which points to an approach which keeps the "natives" in a permanent state of dependence. To be sure, many mission leaders protested against this tendency for local people to become dependent on the mission, but the very approach taken by missions was bound to produce dependency. Such an approach worked from a base of superior power. The missionary was often an employer and sometimes even involved in local government.

The power of the institutional methodology is illustrated by what happened in the Belgian Congo. When Belgium granted Zaire independence in 1960, only a handful of Zairians had graduated from a university. Was this because Zairians are uneducable? Not at all. Their lack of preparation for independence resulted directly from the control of the educational policies by the colonial government, a control reinforced by missions. Missionaries created an extensive educational system in Zaire during the eighty years prior to 1960, but they built it on the assumption that Zairians were not to be trained beyond the secondary level.

Finally, the institutional method highlighted the "foreignness" of these institutions. One must be careful to recognize that institutions as such are not good or bad. Today all the nations of the world affirm the need for schools and hospitals. But to say that the Western pattern for hospitals and schools is the appropriate pattern in all cultures is to ignore the fact that many cultures have for a long time had indigenous institutions for providing medical care and education. Missionary institutions were often introduced into a culture as an alternative to what was already present.

If the word institution describes missionary method in the past, the word *relationship* must describe missionary method in the future. Relationship requires a profound identification with the people among whom the missionary lives and serves. It requires listening to, learning with, depending on, being vulnerable to, becoming interdependent with the host people. The missionary must begin by asking the host people what they want. In the past we have assumed that we knew what was needed, and it was a matter of convincing the people of their need. But this assumption must give way to the more humble approach of being ready to ask what the people perceive their needs to be.

The relational method will avoid exercise of power. We Westerners make our "power" visible through machinery, methods, finance, organization, and personal forcefulness. If we are serious about a method based on relationships, we will insist on letting them build, manage, and own whatever is created.

Mennonite experience since the early 1950s with independent churches in the Argentine Chaco and Africa has taught us how easy it is for us to rob these churches of one of their most important strengths, namely, their self-sufficiency—in economics, in leadership, and in evangelistic outreach. They have not asked us to contribute by remaking them in the image of the mission-established churches. Rather they ask that we capitalize on their indigenous strengths and help them at points of recognized weakness. Specifically they have called for help in Bible study and the training of leaders. To work at this effectively the missionary has had to identify with these churches in their sense of need and resist the temptation to begin immediately to build an institutional complex along conventional lines. The moment missionaries give way to this temptation they begin to undermine these churches at the point of their greatest strength.

To put this matter in a somewhat different perspective, we may characterize this shift in method from institution to relationship in the following way. The institutional method assumed that there were certain defined positions in the various service programs which needed to be filled by workers. To fill these roles the missionary needed the right kind of professional credentials. When we emphasize relationship, the missionary's professional credentials take on secondary importance. The most important credential is whether the missionary wins the confidence and acceptance of the people to whom he or she relates. Such a relationship must be based on love, trust, and mutual respect.

Strategy: From Transplantation to Relationship

Strategy refers to the plan by which objectives are to be achieved. In the past missionary strategy has been geared to the transplantation of the missionary's culture to a new cultural setting. Outwardly, this called for the transfer of organizational forms and institutions from the missionary's culture. Inwardly, it required the transfer of values and attitudes of the missionary's culture. Transplantation involved not simply adding on certain features introduced by missionaries, but displacing traditional values in the receptor culture and substituting for them the missionary's own values. The following diagram helps describe the concept of transplantation:

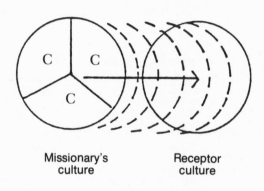

Missionary's culture   Receptor culture

It was not immediately obvious to missionaries that such a transfer of values was evil since many individuals in receptor cultures entered into this process wholeheartedly. Contemporary literature reflects the general revolt against the penetration of Western culture into other parts of the world. But 100 years ago there were Africans, Asians, and others who attempted to become black or Indian "Europeans," in an effort to move up in the world. In the process some people became casualties as they lost their place in traditional society and failed to be completely assimilated into European society.

What is the alternative to transplantation? In our discussion of missionary method we noted that we must make a shift from institution to relationship. Relationship can only be based on sympathetic identification with the people among whom one lives and ministers. The theological term which describes this is incarnation. The coming of Jesus into the world is our model. John says that "the Word became flesh." Incarnation means the self-conscious taking on of the forms of life of a particular culture in order that the gospel may be experienced as the Word of God in that culture.

An incarnational approach does not guarantee that there will be no rejection of the gospel. Scripture tells us that Jesus was perceived as "a stone of stumbling and a rock of offense." His contemporaries executed Him. If the Christian messenger, however, does not undergo this profound identification with the receptor culture, he or she is apt to set up false stones of stumbling so that what people reject is not the true "rock of offense" but idiosyncrasies of the missionary's own culture. Every hearer should be given the opportunity to receive a faithful account of the gospel of Jesus Christ—not a Westernized Jesus.

When we speak about incarnation we must also emphasize the central role of the Holy Spirit as the true leader in mission. Roland Allen, the most important critic of missions in the twentieth century, insisted that the great failure of the modern missionary movement was the way it ignored the foundational role of the Holy Spirit in all missionary undertaking. It is the Spirit who goes before the missionary to prepare the way and then accompanies the missionary in witness. The work of conversion in the heart of the individual is the work of the Spirit—not of missionaries. It is the Holy Spirit who keeps the believer in the faith. From beginning to end missionary witness is the work of the

Holy Spirit. The Spirit is a missionary spirit.

Rather than picturing one culture steamrolling its way over another culture, Scripture describes the coming of the kingdom of God in a quite different way. The gospel is a seed which falls into soil where it germinates and springs to life. The good news of the kingdom begins acting the way leaven permeates dough, quietly but powerfully. It does not displace the dough but rather transforms it into something useful. In this picture the gospel enters a particular human situation both in judgment and in affirmation. It affirms those elements which reflect the Creator's original purposes for humanity; it judges those aspects which express human rebellion against God, and calls all to respond to new life in Christ Jesus.

Role of the Missionary

We have been tracing out major features of the modern missionary movement and the shifts that have occurred over several centuries. We have purposely drawn the picture in black and white—while not losing sight of the introductory comment that basic changes often are incremental and take a long time. The new direction in mission in the future reflects some learning from past experience.

In the past the missionary has been perceived as a "professional" and along with this image went the status and expectations of one who is master. The professional is an expert in a given field by virtue of specialized training and recognition by a professional fraternity. Missionaries also played the role of builder. They often planned and developed educational and medical systems and the auxiliary services that went with those systems. They embodied power and initiative.

Most missionaries in past generations accepted this role without question. It matched the mentality and expectations of the times. But this stance is no longer acceptable. Pressures from two sources demand change, the one external and the other internal: (1) the environment and (2) the biblical view of mission. The world has changed drastically within the past two generations. Colonies have thrown off the yoke of imperialism and claimed their rights to political independence. They have a vision of human dignity and equality which gives hope to many of the world's disenfranchised peoples. A white skin is no longer a credential for special status in the world. Economic power is suspect and resented. Peoples of the world demand respect and mutuality from other peoples.

Of even greater importance, however, is the fact that we have increasingly recognized that the Bible describes the role and stance of the people of God in terms that do not square with the historical image of the missionary. During Jesus' earthly ministry He moved among the people as one who served (Lk. 22:27), and He called His disciples to pattern their ministry after His. The fact that both external pressures and internal logic converge to force a change in missionary stance should help us to accept this change more readily.

The missionary is first and last a servant. Missionaries do not come as those who have rights and prerogatives, but rather as people who are under someone else's command. The missionary is an instrument of the Holy Spirit as the Spirit calls men and women to faith in Jesus Christ. In this sense the missionary is at the disposal of the local church and community.

Missionaries should be present as fellow learners. Not only do they need to learn to understand their adopted people and culture; they need to be part of a local fellowship of believers in a common pilgrimage of faith in obedience to the call of Jesus Christ. Western culture has taught us to believe that the mature person is the one who is self-sufficient and independent, and missionaries have too often reflected this attitude of invulnerability. But Jesus instructed the disciples, whom He commissioned, to adopt a position of vulnerability and dependence in material and spiritual matters. The missionary call is to share life's experiences with the people among whom one lives, without masking or denying personal weakness and need.

In this missionary age the Holy Spirit is calling home the Father's lost sons and daughters. The household of faith is being enlarged as more and more brothers and sisters are brought home. The missionary is appointed to assist these lost ones to find the front door, enter the Father's house, and there to be welcomed to their rightful inheritance.

3
Today's Gospel of Salvation

C. NORMAN KRAUS

Introduction

In January 1973, the Commission on World Mission and Evangelism of the World Council of Churches sponsored a world conference in Bangkok, Thailand, on the theme "Salvation Today." Such a title raises questions. Has the meaning of salvation changed? Is it different today than it was yesterday? And will it be different again tomorrow? Stephen Neill has in fact since published a book entitled *Salvation Tomorrow*, 1976, in which he offers a critique of the salvation today theme. Or was the title intended to emphasize that salvation is a present reality and not just a past event or a future hope? Judging from the reports of the conference both inferences were intended. The concept of salvation today is contextually different than yesterday because of a vastly changed world; and salvation must be taken seriously as a present, historical reality.

The question of what it means to proclaim Christ as

C. Norman Kraus was until 1979 director of the Center for Discipleship and a professor at Goshen College, Goshen, Indiana. The author of several books, he is presently a missionary in Japan.

"Savior of the world" has been raised anew in our generation by the convergence of a number of revolutionary factors. It is difficult to know exactly how and if these factors
are causally related. Perhaps they are just convergent, but in
any case they create a new situation in which the question of
the meaning and implications of salvation for today must be
seriously reexamined. This has been recognized by Evangelicals and ecumenicals alike.[1]

Changed Concept of the World

The first of these factors which makes a reexamination of
the concept of salvation necessary is the changed concept of
the world. Our view has changed both politically and re-
ligiously. Until the present generation in the West we have
viewed the world as partly civilized and partly uncivilized.
Naturally we considered ourselves the civilized! And being
civilized we assumed the right and even the responsibility to
dominate other people and nations. This was the mandate or
"burden" which "Christian" privilege laid upon us.[2] So the
world was divided into the self-determining, ruler nations
and their dependent colonies called "protectorates"; salvation was associated with civilization and upward socioeconomic movement. This has drastically changed. Now small-
ness and technological underdevelopment no longer auto-
matically give powerful nations the moral right to control or
dominate. The political fact of the United Nations where
large and small nations cooperate in mutual respect is a
remarkable symbol of this new political reality. Further, we
are far less certain that salvation can be identified with
technical and social progress.

The events in China at the present moment dramatically
illustrate this new reality in the world. In the nineteenth
century China was considered a backward nation and forced

to open its doors to trade and missionaries. It fought back, for example, in the Boxer Rebellion of 1900, but the Western powers held on. Then China drove out her imperialist rulers following World War II in a communistic revolution and asserted her own identity and right to self-determination. In so doing she also expelled all missionaries and opted for a secular way of salvation. Now that she has achieved independence and identity she is reestablishing her ties with those who earlier dominated her. What will a proclamation of salvation mean in the China of today and tomorrow now that salvation can no longer be thought of as part of the civilization process offered by a superior culture to inferior cultures?

For religious purposes the world was divided into Christian and non-Christian or "heathen" nations, and the message of salvation was carried from the Christian nations to the heathen nations. Western Christian civilization was considered to be the direct product of revelation and thus unique and superior to all other religions. The *gospel* was virtually equated with the religious and moral values of Western Christianity, and conversion meant making a radical cultural change. Heathenism was considered simply the work of the devil which should be displaced by Christianity. Salvation meant the acceptance of the Christian religion along with its implied culture.

Now we are much more hesitant to identify any civilization or nation as Christian. The West is far more secular than Christian. At most, it is highly pluralistic. And Western Christianity is recognized to be a particular cultural version of the biblical faith. We cannot equate gospel and Western Christianity. What is the content of a message of salvation separated from the gospel of Western civilization and technology?

Neither do we think of national cultures which are dominated by other ideologies or religions as "heathen," that is, the work of the devil in contrast to Christian culture. The devil does not create culture, humans do. All cultures are *human* cultures. Therefore they are *all* fallible and sinful including Christian culture. The devil sees to that! Thus people in all cultures and nations need the message of salvation; and that message calls all people, including Christians, to repentance.

The church now exists in all different kinds of cultures across national boundaries as a witness to God's salvation. The message of salvation has been embodied in a plurality of cultural patterns. Thus it can no longer be thought of as the message from a superior civilization or religion to an inferior one. Rather than simply calling for the destruction and displacement of an inferior "heathen culture" the message must speak to the redemption of a people's cultural values and expressions.

New Anthropological Knowledge

The new anthropological insights which have changed our perceptions of the missionary's approach and task are a second change factor.[3] Anthropological studies have changed our understanding of the communication process; our approach to translation of the Bible from the careful word for word equivalence to dynamic cultural equivalence of meaning; our ideas about the cultural aspects of conversion to Christ; and our evaluation of many strange customs and practices. It has taught us how intricate are the connections between individual persons and their social tradition. And it has helped us to see that every human culture is a potential vehicle to carry the good news of God's salvation. It has raised in a new way the question of how salvation is related to the plurality of human cultures, and whether the goal of salvation is one great homogeneous multitude which incidentally looks more Western than African or Asian. What will be the cultural complexion of "that great multitude which no man could number, from every nation, from all tribes and peoples and tongues, standing before the throne and before the Lamb clothed in white robes ..."? (Rev. 7:9-10).

Biblical Interpretation

A third major change factor is our understanding of the Bible itself.[4] We have come to see that the Bible on its human side is a multicultural document. It represents the interaction of God and the changing Israelite culture over at least a 1,500-year period. Written in three languages it reflects the major shift from Israelite to Jewish self-consciousness in the second and first centuries BC, and the crossing from a Judaic cultural setting to Hellenism in the first century AD. Its languages and thought forms reflect a historical dialogue with the nations that surrounded Palestine and at times overran it.

This new perspective on Scripture calls for a new approach to interpretation. In brief it calls for a cumulative approach to understanding a concept like salvation which helps us to appreciate its varied and complementary meanings. Understandings of salvation developed in a historical context as God revealed Himself more fully to His people. Along the way new dimensions of meaning added a profuse richness to the concept, but we have tended to slough off older materialistic and corporate meanings on the assumption that the new spiritual insights superseded the old. We have spiritualized the Old Testament meanings in light of certain key New Testament references to salvation as a re-

stored spiritual relation of the individual to God. Rather than
to treat the biblical material cumulatively, adding meaning
to meaning, we substitute the latter for the former. Now in
light of the worldwide multicultural missionary activity as
well as the biblical research of the past one hundred years
this rationalistic and spiritualizing way of interpreting Scripture must be challenged.

Missionary Experience

One last factor to be mentioned is the experience of sensitive missionaries and evangelists. Here we can take examples
from the home front as well as the foreign field. Evangelists
like Tom Skinner and John Perkins who have worked among
the poor and exploited blacks soon found that preaching
Christ required more than evangelistic meetings to inspire
spiritual decisions for Christ. Tom began talking about saving "persons," not "souls," and his associate William Pan-
nell wrote about the necessary close integration of social and
civil action with evangelism as a part of the work of salvation.

John Perkins began as an evangelistic preacher in the
black high schools of Mississippi, but he soon found himself
immersed in the civil rights struggle for freedom *as an evangelist.* In recent years he has become deeply involved in raising the physical, intellectual, and economic standards of
Mississippi blacks.

In the third world, that is, countries mostly of the
southern hemisphere which are economically poor and
technologically less developed, missionary strategies are
increasingly including programs for economic and social
development, and justice. These are not merely an entice-
ment to conversion of individuals, but an integrated part of
their witness to God's salvation.

One of the most forthright theological restatements of salvation as inclusive of both social and spiritual deliverance is the so-called "liberation theology." South American theologians of both Roman Catholic and Protestant persuasion have defined salvation as liberation of people from spiritual, political, and socioeconomic bondage. They point out that Jesus preached "good news to the poor" and used His power to set them free. In a similar identification with the poor they are attempting to understand the mission of the church as a witness to salvation.

Orlando Costas, an evangelical theologian who identifies with this train of thought has written:

> The Church is faithful to her witnessing vocation when she becomes a catalyst for God's liberating action in the world of poverty, exploitation, hunger, guilt and despair by standing in solidarity with people, by showing them with concrete actions that God cares and wills to save them and by helping them to understand the material and moral roots of their situation. The Church is faithful to her task of bringing good news of salvation when she relates the meaning of Christ to the history of mankind; when she interprets the history of the peoples of the various cultures of the earth in the light of the comprehensive meaning of the Gospel; and when, specifically and concretely, she confronts each member of her surrounding neighboring communities with the claims of Christ upon his life and thus makes the Gospel pertinent to his particular life situation."[5]

Salvation Today

When we reflected on the title "Salvation Today" we raised the question whether the concept of salvation has changed. In truth, it has. Eastern (Greek) and Western (Latin) Christianity have different conceptions, and a succession of concepts have evolved within the Western church itself. Indeed, a reconceptualization of salvation lay at the roots of the Protestant rejection of the Roman church in the sixteenth century.

According to Protestant reformers salvation was understood as forgiveness of sins and justification of the sinner before God. The guilt and spiritual consequences of sins are removed in the experience of salvation. The social consequences of this theological readjustment were hotly debated. Would there be discernable consequences—new lifestyles, a new visible community? If so, were these consequences part of the salvation itself? Might one speak of persons being saved even where they were not present? By and large, Orthodoxy opted to separate salvation by faith from any form of "good works" as part of the transaction itself. Pietism of the seventeenth and eighteenth centuries corrected Orthodoxy to some extent when it insisted that personal morality and social concern are integral to true spirituality.

But it was only in modern Liberalism that a genuinely social gospel was developed, that is, a concept of salvation which was not confined to the individual's spiritual relation to God. There were real problems with many of Liberalism's theological definitions, but on this point it moved the church's self-understanding toward a more biblical position. And now today we can only rejoice that a large segment of Evangelicalism is recovering the social dimensions of the biblical message of salvation.

The Bangkok conference, which followed several years of study on the theme, attempted to enunciate a concept of salvation which "offers a comprehensive wholeness in this divided life."[6] Its major task was to explore the relation of salvation to creation, that is, to history, society, and culture in general. Affirming that God the Creator is also God the Redeemer, and that it is precisely the creation, both mankind and nature, that is to be "recreated," they explored

what it means for the life and mission of the church to proclaim salvation in Christ.

After the initial addresses the conference was divided into
three sections. One section discussed salvation and culture.
This question is important because human beings are creatures of culture, and they receive their self-identity through
interaction and conditioning within a given culture. How
then does conversion change one's relation to culture? Does
individual salvation necessitate transferring one's cultural
allegiance from a "non-Christian" to a "Christian" culture?
Should the saved community think of itself as a countercul-
ture? How does salvation affect one's cultural roles—sex,
class, caste, family, business roles, for examples.

Another group examined the "nature of the mission of
God and the obedience of the churches."[7] This section dealt
with the way in which the church bears witness to salvation
in its own life and in its proclamation to the world.

Section II discussed salvation and social justice. This
group looked at the salvation process primarily as a social-
historical process. Assuming that Christ is the Lord of history, and that He is working out His plan in history until "he
has put all his enemies under his feet" (1 Corinthians 15:25),
they concluded that the present-day struggle for liberation
and justice must have some salvific significance. This group
asked what that significance might be, and how Christians
in mission should relate to the struggle for human dignity,
economic justice, meaning, and hope in this life.

Only this section attempted a theological statement on
the meaning of salvation, and it is worth quoting in part:

> The salvation which Christ brought, and in which we par-
> ticipate, offers a comprehensive wholeness in this divided life.
> We understand salvation as newness of life—the unfolding of

true humanity in the fulness of God (Colossians 2:9). It is a salvation of the soul and the body, of the individual and society, mankind and the "groaning creation" (Romans 8:19). As evil works both in personal life and in exploitative social structures which humiliate humankind, so God's justice manifests itself both in the justification of the sinner and in social and political justice. As guilt is both individual and corporate so God's liberating power changes both persons and structures. We have to overcome the dichotomies in our thinking between soul and body, person and society, humankind and creation. Therefore we see the struggles for economic justice, political freedom and cultural renewal as elements in the total liberation of the world through the mission of God. . . . [8]

It is clear then that "salvation today" means salvation *in* history. Although they speak of the culmination when "death is swallowed up in victory" (1 Corinthians 15:54), a concept that takes us beyond our present earthly existence, the major stress falls on salvation as present reality. Further, present historical reality means a holistic—social, individual, spiritual, psychological, and material—healing of our lives. Thus they call for a mission strategy that takes seriously the concrete situations of our lives, that is, "economic justice, political freedom, and cultural renewal," and not merely a theologically abstracted justification.[9] What shall we say in response to such a concept? How does it measure up to the biblical concepts of salvation?

Biblical Meanings of Salvation

I shall not attempt a definitive treatment of the meaning of salvation in the Bible, but rather call our attention to some crucial aspects of the biblical concept and trace some of its richness of meaning in the New Testament as it develops from the Old. I am assuming that the Old Testament is the proper background and context against which the New is to be understood and that the conception of salvation is a cumulative one.

Salvation a Present Reality

In the first place, the words for salvation in both the Old and New Testaments indicate a rescue from peril, destruction, or defeat by an enemy. The Exodus, as has often been pointed out, becomes the model for salvation in Israel. God is Israel's Savior because He delivered them from Pharaoh and by a miraculous escape brought them to Sinai where they were formed into a covenant people. Thus salvation has a historical meaning for the biblical writers. It is something God has done and continues to do for Israel in their life under His covenant.

Alan Richardson contrasts such a historical concept of salvation with philosophical ideas: " . . . the biblical doctrine of salvation is not a theory or set of ideas about God; it is not a logical deduction from theistic philosophy; nor yet is it based upon any technique of mystical absorption into the divine. Biblical theology is essentially recital . . . the biblical doctrine of salvation is an assertion of something which actually happened."[10] That happenedness is what we mean by historical.

To underscore, salvation was not thought of as an escape from the material world of evil and sin into a spiritual paradise. In its biblical setting salvation is first deliverance in the world from present evil whether natural (famine and plague), social (war and oppression), or spiritual (sin and its personal consequences). It was conceived as an actual event in history. In the long development of the biblical concept, salvation never lost this fundamental temporal orientation although it added other dimensions of meaning.

According to the Gospels, Jesus came announcing a new

present reality—the arrival of the kingdom or rule of God.
This rule of God, which is a synonym for "the salvation of
God," was manifested in the ministry of Jesus when in the
power of the Spirit He overcame the powers of evil. He
healed the sick and freed those held in demonic bondage.
He forgave and reconciled sinners, restored joy and purpose
to lives, released the destitute from the anxiety and
depression of poverty, and delivered the rich from the pride
and alienation of riches. His call was to repentance, the
reorientation of life in society; and this was to be a present
historical reality.

In the Pauline Epistles salvation in Christ is described as
deliverance from sin and the powers of death, and again this
is not understood simply in spiritual or theological terms. It
is a social, historical deliverance. Salvation is liberation from
the frustration of indecision and moral impotence (Romans
7—8). It is freedom from bondage to cultural traditions and
values which inhibit meaningful social change (Galatians
3:26-28; Colossians 3:1). It is deliverance from self-centered-
ness that makes personal fulfilment and wholeness in loving
relations possible (Galatians 2:20). It frees from the guilt,
fear, and self-depreciation that often bind us in physical and
mental illness. Orlando Costas sums it up as follows:

> In the New Testament salvation has at least a threefold
> meaning: (1) liberation from the power of sin and death
> (Romans 8:1-2), (2) being born into the family of God (John
> 1:12; Romans 8:6, 17, 29; Galatians 3:16, 26-29; 4:5b-7; 1 John
> 2:1-2), (3) participation in the reign of Christ (cf. Ephesians
> 1:20 ff.; 2:6; Revelation 1:5 f.). Understood thus, salvation "of-
> fers a comprehensive wholeness in this divided life."[11]

Again, while this fuller understanding of salvation fills the
concept with new personal and social dimensions, it does not

remove it from the historical realm. It is not abstracted, mythologized, or theologized. It remains a present reality.

A Social-Personal Reality

A second aspect of the biblical concept of salvation which we need to highlight is its essentially social character. The formation of the "mixed multitude" of slaves that left Egypt (Exodus 12:38, RSV) into a new cohesive community of free, self-governing people under the rule of Yahweh was a fundamental part of their salvation. That is the significance of the covenant at Sinai. That covenant given to them by God gave them their self-identity as Yahweh's people. To be saved meant to accept His name and come under His authority. It meant to belong to this redeemed people. Salvation was literally to be found *in community*.

In the New Testament there is no essential change in this social dimension of salvation. Under the new covenant salvation meant to accept the name and authority of Jesus as the Lord of the new community. Thus salvation is said to be in the name of Jesus, and only in His name. The new disciple band was soon to be called "Christians" (Acts 11:26).[12]

What is changed in the New Testament is the nature of the community, and thus the self-identity of the saved individual. The new community is a fellowship of the Spirit rather than a nation under law. Its individual members are given their identity as children in the family of God by His Spirit (Romans 8:15). They are motivated by the love of Christ rather than legal precepts. They are caught up in His messianic mission, and in that mission they receive their salvation.

Such an understanding of the community under Christ's lordship and saviorhood gives new depth to the significance of individuality and of individual salvation. In the community or "body of Christ" each member is saved by Christ. Each individual is ultimately responsible to Christ, the "Head" (1 Corinthians 4:1-4). Each individual receives nourishment and guidance from Christ, the Spirit (Ephesians 4:15b-16); and each is responsible for his or her gift given by the Spirit. But this is not independent of the body of Christ. Salvation is not *by* or through the church; it is *by* Christ *in* the church.

Note the following: The New Testament phrases "in Christ," "in the name of Christ," "in the body of Christ" are often used synonymously. To be "baptized into Christ" or "incorporated into Christ" are ways of speaking about the salvation experience (Romans 6:3-6). Being baptized into Christ and into the body of Christ (cf. 1 Corinthians 12:13, 27; Galatians 3:27) or "in the name of the Lord Jesus" (Acts 2:38; 8:12; 19:5) are obviously not references to different baptisms, but to the one baptism viewed from different perspectives. Thus we can only conclude that from the New Testament viewpoint the "in Christ" experience of salvation is inherently a social experience.

Salvation as Reconciliation

Perhaps the most characteristic meaning of salvation in Scripture is expressed in the language of reconciliation and peace. Indeed, the "peace of God" and the "salvation of God" are synonyms in the thought of the prophets. Humanity's alienation and hostility toward God and each other causes their self-destruction. "The wages of sin is death" (Romans 6:23). But God's gracious act of forgiveness and reconciliation saves them from destruction and restores the possibility of eternal life in fellowship with Himself.

Salvation is thus described as the peace (*shalom*) of God, both individual and social, that flows from God's forgiveness and reconciliation. In Romans 5:1-11 the emphasis is upon the reconciliation between the individual and God—"peace with God." We are, says Paul, "justified," "reconciled," and "saved" from God's wrath, that is, the inexorable consequences of sin unrepented of, through the death and resurrection of Christ (vv. 9-10). Even in this passage which so beautifully describes the new relationship of individuals with God, Paul clearly has in mind more than the individual's private spiritual "peace with God." His mind is on the solidarity of mankind in sin and the effect of Christ's reconciling death for all mankind (5:18-19). Reconciliation has horizontal human dimensions as well as vertical spiritual ones.

Paul understood this reconciliation process to have already begun as a result of Christ's death and resurrection. Through His cross which did away with the demands of the Mosaic law He made peace between Jews and Gentiles (Ephesians 2:11 ff.). That law had been regarded by Israel as the symbol of her moral superiority in the ancient world. It was the mark of her distinctive national existence as "God's people." Thus it had become divisive and alienating. Now, Paul says, those who had been aliens are included in the covenant of promise and have been made "fellow citizens" and "members of the household of God" (2:19). This new standing in God's sight and purpose marks the possibility of a new reconciled humanity where the old walls of discrimination and hostility are broken down (vv. 14-16). And this new salvation began in the church as the new people of God.

In the New Testament where the nationalistic features of peoplehood are dropped those being saved are described as a community of persons who share one life and purpose in Christ (Acts 4:32). Their new identity as the family of God through Jesus Christ (Ephesians 2:19), or their new allegiance to the "kingdom [of God] and his righteousness"

(Matthew 6:33), restores that social unity and transcendent purpose which gives human existence its true dignity and worth (Galatians 3:26-28). Or to put it yet another way, it brings to fruition the original intention of God in the creation. In that sense salvation is spoken of as a "recreation" of humanity in the image of God "in true righteousness and holiness" (Ephesians 4:24).

The Eschatological Dimension

In the biblical concept of salvation as a present reality there is always an element of incompletion and process which points toward a future fulfillment. The nature of the end *(eschatos)* is revealed in what has happened and is happening, but it is only pointed to and not fully realized. This is the eschatological dimension of salvation. Salvation in history is never finalized and complete. We are "saved in hope" (Romans 8:24).

This is true both for the individual and society. We do not know perfection, not even in love, as Wesley taught. There is no "entire sanctification" for individuals. Neither do we enjoy or expect the total achievement of social justice—the sanctification of the social order—in our present existence. Nevertheless these hopes remain the expected culmination. And we are confidently aware that their fulfillment is already in process because of the resurrection and because of the Spirit of Jesus which has been given to us. Thus Jesus' command to "seek first the rule of God and his righteousness" is no invitation to frustration!

In the Old Testament the prophets of Israel looked for a consumation in "the day of the Lord," when He would judge in righteousness and purify the "sons of Jacob." This was a fulfillment that would establish a permanent peace of God under the righteous judgment of the "Son of David." It would be not only a time of social justice and equity, but of reconciliation between nature, the animal kingdom, and mankind (Isaiah 11:1-9). At that future time, Isaiah prophesied, Israel would say,

> Behold, God is my salvation;
> I will trust, and will not be afraid;
> for the Lord God is my strength and my song,
> and he has become my salvation (12:2).

Again the New Testament picks up and expands this eschatological theme. Peter speaks of this ultimate salvation as "now in readiness to be revealed in the last time" when Jesus will be "revealed" as the Lord of the universe. Now, he says, we have the "salvation of . . . [our] souls" in faith and hope (1 Peter 1:5-9).

The ultimate goal of salvation is the reunifying of the whole universe in Christ—"things in heaven and things on earth" (Ephesians 1:10; Colossians 1:19-20). Now our salvation is in process, and we wait along with all creation for our destiny as the family of God to be revealed. Even though we already have received the Spirit of true paternity we groan in pain and labor for the birth of a new creation (Romans 8:18-25; 2 Corinthians 5:1-5). Although we experience physical preservation and renewal, yet we live with weakness and must submit to death, the "last enemy," to be conquered by Christ. Already the "new creation" is in formation, and those who are united to Christ have begun to live in the new order.[13]

This salvation process is not only going on in the life of individuals, but is also moving forward in the social process. God is reconciling mankind to Himself and to each other through the cross of Christ by forming them into one new community under His new covenant. Through the reign of

the resurrected Christ He is overcoming the principalities
and powers that have perpetuated the bondage of creation
(Ephesians 2:20-22; Colossians 2:15; 1 Corinthians 15:24-
25). According to His agelong purpose (Ephesians 3:11) He
is forming "one new humanity" in Christ.

We do not fully understand how the end which will be
the work of God is related to the historical process now in
progress. We cannot comprehend how the historical is related to that which is beyond history. Shall we view salvation
history in apocalyptic millennialistic categories? Or are
developmental categories more adequate? Will Christ build
His rule of salvation (kingdom) on the failure of human efforts? There are biblical passages that strongly indicate this
approach. Or will the rule of God spread as ferment in
dough, or grow as an undetected plant until it dominates the
world scene? Some parables of Jesus suggest this approach.
We do not know the final answers to these questions, nor do
we need to know. Yet we look for a consummation of history
which at the same time fulfills and transcends it.

What is of fundamental importance is a clear understanding of the *goal* of salvation. That goal is *the formation of the
new humanity*. And this goal is the same both in and beyond
history. The new humanity is already in formation. Jesus
Christ is the "pioneer" and heavenly prototype. His Spirit
has been given to the community and to individuals in it as a
seal and guarantee of the fulfillment of the new reality. The
"body of Christ" is the firstfruits of the new order in the
midst of the old. And when Jesus, the Son of God, is
revealed, we know that we shall be made in His image. That
will be the consummation of our salvation.

We believe according to the revelation given to us in
Christ's death and resurrection that the transcendent end
stands in continuity with our present experience of God as

Savior. We "work out . . . [our] salvation" confident that it is God who is at work in us to accomplish His good pleasure (Philippians 2:12b-13). Thus we are convinced that proclamation of the gospel is an integral part of salvation history, and that our work is not in vain in the Lord.

Contemporary Good News

If the biblical concept of salvation has been correctly highlighted, how shall we translate it in our modern world? How shall we contextualize it? Let me offer four guidelines.

First, the message of salvation must be good news for individuals. In our concern to recognize the social aspects of salvation, we must not fall into the error of collectivism which nullifies the unique significance of the individual. On the other hand, to take individuals seriously is to take them in their social setting. To be saved is to be saved in our relationships to others—to be reconciled.

Further, we said that the message must be *good news*. So often the gospel is presented as a new demand—"the demands of the gospel." How can we rephrase in *gospel* language that oft-heard shibboleth? We shift the order of priority in the "fruit of the Spirit" to read "self-control, patience, goodness. . . ." We begin with the moral imperative rather than the joyous, liberating news indicative of God's love. The only "demand" of the gospel is to truly repent, which means to accept the good news and submit to God's love.

The gospel is good news of *liberation*. This is the ringing message of Galatians. "For freedom Christ has set us free" (5:1). Free from fear because there is no fear in love. Free from the "powers" of self and society which bind us and inhibit our best intentions. Free to be what God made us to be.

It is the good news of *reconciliation*. The reconciliation to ourselves that comes from knowing that God has made us acceptable in Christ; and that peace with our fellows which is only possible to those who are at peace with God and themselves.

It is the promise of *personal fulfillment* as children of God which His Spirit already certifies to us in the restoration of wholeness and joy. And it is the *new life* and *empowerment* from God. As Paul put it, it is knowing the strength of God in our weakness.

Last, it is the endowment of life with *hope* and *real meaning* which gives worth to even the banalities of existence. In sum it is God giving Himself to us for the true fulfillment of life called "eternal life" in the Gospel of John.

Second, a historical salvation must be salvation in context. The good news of salvation must offer solutions for real, concrete (contextual) sins, fears, and bondage. We should not try to save people from other people's sins or to project guilt so that we can offer a remedy. The angel's message to Joseph was that Mary's son should be called Jesus because He would save His people from "their sins." Perhaps we should not press the text too far, but it is clear that Jesus was first of all a Savior to His own people dealing with their needs before He was Savior of the world.

The cultural manifestations of sin are multifold even though the primal causes are the same, and the gospel addresses itself to both manifestation and cause. If the problem is a deep sense of guilt and despair, the gospel offers forgiveness, acceptance, and a new possibility. Where the problem surfaces as bondage and fear of demons the good news is of a greater power which is victorious over the power of evil. Incidentally, there are more examples of exorcism in the Gospels than of forgiveness! If the bondage is to tradition personified in ancestors, or to fate and the law of *karma* that undercuts motivation and inhibits social improvement, the good news is of a personal God who stands before us in the future and beckons us to the attainment of "eternal life."

To those in hunger and poverty, the good news speaks not only of the riches of a spiritual kingdom, but of dignity as God's beloved children and of bread which the Father has provided for all of them. To those in prison it means liberation and rehabilitation. And where hostility, discrimination, and exploitation abound, it is the gospel of peace.

The contextualization of salvation also means that persons are offered salvation in their own cultural setting. This is the essential implication of salvation through incarnation. To be biblical our concept of salvation must relate to the cultural identity of those to whom it is offered. Salvation is to conform us to the image of God's Son not to some other person's cultural image, for example, the missionary's. In this sense the message of salvation must be an African, Latino, Philippino, black, American gospel.

Third, a biblical concept of salvation must speak to the social or corporate realities of human life. It must take seriously the fact that we are intrinsically social creatures and cannot be saved in segregation from our social context. The final goal of God's mission is a redeemed human society at peace with itself and its cosmic environment—"a new heaven and earth in which dwells righteousness"—and not simply the escape of a few selected individuals from an unsalvageable world.

Our theological understanding of salvation since the Reformation has been largely in terms of the justification and sanctification of individuals. In the Protestant restatement salvation was spiritualized and theologized. This was especially true in the strictly orthodox tradition of Protestantism where salvation was virtually identified with belief in correct doctrine. In the nonmillennialist interpretation of God's plan for history even the kingdom of God, a social concept, was spiritualized. In the premillennial schools of thought it was relegated to an apocalyptic future that was virtually disconnected from the present salvation of God.

Biblical thought relates salvation to the social goals of the kingdom of God. As we have seen, in Galatians 3:26-27 Paul clearly and deliberately joins the "in Christ" concept with the realization of a social-psychological community. In Christ there is neither Jew nor Greek, slave nor free, male nor female. And in the parallel passage of Colossians 3:10-11 this same social reality is the outcome of having "put on the new nature, which is being renewed in knowledge after the image of its creator." Further, in Ephesians and Colossians Christ's work in death and resurrection is immediately related to the "principalities and powers" which control social and political life in this age. Christ has disarmed and exposed them on the cross (Colossians 2:15). His plan of salvation is to be made known to them (Ephesians 3:10). And in 1 Corinthians 15:24-25 Christ is even now in the process of putting all His enemies under His feet. In all these pivotal passages, salvation clearly has a broad sociopolitical reference.

The last guideline is that authentic witness to biblical salvation must include the actual signs of the new order among us in communities of salvation. There must be the demonstration of salvation in process in communities of repentance that function as salt and light in the world. It is important to speak of the future consummation of salvation when death is destroyed and the whole creation is renewed after the image of Christ. But this understanding is not enough. A present community in which the new order of creation is already begun, where personal life is renewed and relationships are restored under the lordship of Christ is both a witnessing sign and a new beginning process.

Our theological concept of salvation is closely related to our understanding of the church's mission in the world. What goals and strategy should we pursue in bearing witness to God's salvation? It has been my concern in this chapter that we think carefully about our doctrine as we reshape our practice of evangelization.

4

An Evangelistic Lifestyle for the Congregation

HOWARD A. SNYDER

In an article in the November 1978 issue of the Southern Baptist publication *Home Missions*, Toby Druin attempts to guage the effectiveness of the nationwide "Here's Life, America" campaign and the similar statewide "Good News Texas" campaign sponsored by Southern Baptists in 1977. The report raises issues which provide a good starting point for considering the question of an evangelistic lifestyle for the congregation.[1]

"Here's Life, America" was a multimillion dollar evangelistic effort sponsored by Campus Crusade for Christ, localized in 253 metropolitan areas in the United States. It involved over 14,500 local churches, and three fourths of all Americans were said to have been exposed to the campaign's catchy "I Found It" slogan during the campaign. (The "I Found It" bumper stickers provoked some counter-stickers, including "I Gave It Back" and the Jewish response, "We Never Lost It!") "Here's Life, World" is now projected by

Howard A. Snyder of Winona Lake, Indiana, is executive director of Light and Life Men International. He is author of *The Problem of Wineskins* (Inter-Varsity Press, 1975) and *The Community of the King* (Inter-Varsity Press, 1977).

Campus Crusade at a cost of some $1 billion.

"Good News Texas" was a smaller-scale but similar evangelistic effort costing over $1 million and aimed at evangelizing 4.7 million unchurched Texans during the spring and summer of 1977. Local church campaigns were backed up by a media blitz including radio and TV testimonials by famous personalities on 300 stations, 1,700 billboards, and extensive newspaper advertising. A secular advertising agency helped design and carry out the campaign. Reliable estimates indicate that more than half of all Texans saw the TV spots, and of these, one third said their attitudes toward religion had been changed. Media people say this response was a "significant achievement."

Probably all of us have been aware of the "Here's Life" campaign, and some of our churches may have participated in it. A number of churches in my denomination were rather heavily involved, and one of our larger Indianapolis churches was used by Campus Crusade as a "model" in promoting "Here's Life" in other cities. Some of our churches report that they benefited from the endeavor.

It seems to me that the unprecedented "Here's Life" effort may represent a significant turning point for North American evangelical churches. This effort, in retrospect, may mark the point, not where North American churches took a quantum leap forward in evangelism, but where they finally learned that evangelism will fail if it does not grow out of the integrity and spiritual vitality of the local congregation.

All indications are that "Here's Life" was a great media success and a drastic evangelistic failure. The same is true of the "Good News Texas" campaign. Millions of Americans "heard" the message and were "influenced" by it. These campaigns may even have produced some good in the form of pre-evangelism. But all empirical studies so far yield the same result: Thousands of "decisions" but only the tiniest trickle of new church members. And the evidence suggests that most "converts" represent Christian rededications and transfers from one church to another.

James Engel notes that of the more than one half million persons who claimed they had received Christ through "Here's Life," fewer than 3 percent became church members (citing Peter Wagner's study). Further, notes Engel,

> ... it was contended that 175 million people were exposed to the claims of the gospel. Because of media saturation, this figure could be accurate, but exposure and comprehension are very different matters. In a survey undertaken at the Wheaton Graduate School it was discovered that about eighty percent of those living in Upper Arlington, Ohio (a wealthy suburb of Columbus), indeed were aware of the "I found it" theme, but only forty percent understood the message. And at least half of this forty percent were already Christian or Christian-oriented. The great majority never comprehended what it was trying to say.[2]

The problem is compounded by the extravagant claims made for "Here's Life" by Bill Bright and others. Bright said at the outset of "Here's Life" that the campaign "may very well determine both the destiny of our nation and the future of all civilization." He was quoted as saying in 1976, " 'Here's Life, America' is the greatest spiritual harvest in the history of the church—100 times, yes, 1,000 times greater than anything I have ever seen or read about. I believe one can truthfully say here in the United States the Great Commission will be fulfilled. ..."[3]

Such statements and subsequent claims regarding "Here's Life" create a tremendous credibility gap. As studies by Win Arn and others have shown, "Here's Life" has had virtually no measurable impact on church membership in the United States.[4] We may hope that it has had some significant, less tangible results, and that it may have contributed in some way to a broad-based spiritual awakening in America. But all indications are that its impact will have been primarily on some of the individual Christians and local churches which participated, not on the mass of North American pagans "Here's Life" was intended to have reached.

In fact, "Here's Life" is going the way of "Key '73," Evangelism in Depth, and similar efforts before it. George Peters (in *Saturation Evangelism*) and Peter Wagner (in *Frontiers in Missionary Strategy*) have shown that Evangelism in Depth had little real impact in terms of church growth, and that the major reason was that the effort did not grow naturally out of the normal life of local congregations.[5] This fact suggests that an ecclesiological issue is at stake.[6]

The major argument for such intensive evangelistic campaigns as Evangelism in Depth and "Here's Life" is, of course, that the local churches "aren't getting the job done." Churches are failing in their evangelism. Therefore a large-scale, broad-based, intensive effort sponsored by some outside or overarching entity is needed to do the job, bring in the harvest, and give churches a much needed shot of adrenalin.

But the neglected issue here is the question of the nature of the church itself. The failure of "Here's Life" and similar efforts is not, fundamentally, a technical or programming failure. The problem goes deeper than the question of methods. It is time to stop talking about programming mistakes or faulty techniques and face up to a fundamental theological error concerning the nature of the church and therefore the nature of salvation itself. The truth is that no one can be joined to Christ the Head without being joined to Christ's body, and the error is to think, first, that a person can become a Christian without being born into God's family in a visible way, and, second, that evangelism can be authentic while ignoring this dynamic relationship of Head and body.

We need to recover the classical doctrine that "Outside the church there is no salvation"—but understood biblically. Augustine was right to emphasize the close, inseparable relationship of Head and body in the church. He was right to say the history of the church parallels the history of Christ, the Head. The problem with the classical view of "no salvation outside the church" is that this came to be understood institutionally and sacramentally rather than in terms of vital, visible participation in the community of God's people where intimate fellowship with God is joined with intimate fellowship with the brothers and sisters who make up Christ's body.

We have tended to think institutionally, rather than communally, about the church. Our conceptions have often been technical rather than charismatic; organizational rather than organic. Strangely, this has been true in the present age even in churches which stand in the Anabaptist and believers' church tradition—a witness to the pervasive influence of contemporary North American society. No wonder Third World evangelical Christians are nervous about the exportation of American church growth technology![7] They perceive quite correctly that underlying issues of discipleship and church integrity are at stake, and have not adequately been dealt with on the North American scene.

Many reasons may be cited for our failures in evangelism, and all these should be examined.[8] But my argument here is that evangelistic effectiveness begins with proper attention to the life and integrity of the congregation. This, then, will be the focus of the following observations.

The Life-Sharing Community

Evangelism always has been and always will be an important priority of any biblically based church. This priority is not first of all because of a concern for growth but because the church is called to participate in the mission of God. The kingdom of God incorporates "all things" (Ephesians 1:10), but it centers in the allegiance of individual wills and lives to the Person and lordship of Jesus Christ. The church has an exclusive biblical mandate for proclamation, persuasion evangelism, informal sharing of the good news, and incorporating new believers into the life of the Christian community.

Beyond the fact of biblical mandate, however, is simply the impulse of Pentecost—the motivating power of love and joy in Christian lives which, by the agency of the Holy Spirit, impels Christians gladly to share what they have discovered with those who remain in darkness. Thus evangelism still is "one beggar telling another where to find bread."

Seven propositions, it seems to me, are important in developing an evangelistic lifestyle for the congregation. These affirmations are based on the assumption that evangelism is a proper priority for the congregation, but that this priority fits integrally into a web of intertwined priorities to be controlled by the fundamental calling of the church to glorify God and participate in His mission.

1. *The church's first concern in evangelism is to participate in the mission of God—to do the works of Christ and work for the progressive manifestation of His reign.*

Jesus said His disciples would continue His work and

would "do even greater things than these, because I am going to the Father" (John 14:12).° I take it that the "greater works" referred to here by Jesus do not involve primarily more dramatic or more powerful feats, but rather the extension of Jesus' ministry "into all the world" through the church. The reason Jesus' disciples will do "greater works" is that Jesus is going to the Father. Jesus spoke this in the context of repeated references to the Holy Spirit. He said, "It is for your good that I am going away. Unless I go away, the Counselor will not come to you; but if I go, I will send him to you" (John 16:7). The Spirit, says Jesus, "will testify about me; but you also must testify, for you have been with me from the beginning" (John 15:26-27).

Jesus came to do the work of the Father. He accomplished the work given Him to do while physically present on earth. With His death and resurrection comes a new phase of His work. Before His resurrection, Jesus was limited by space and time. The body of Christ was a physical, space-time body like yours and mine. But that body was broken on the cross so that salvation could be manifested and the church could be born. In the same way that bread was broken and multiplied in the feeding of the thousands, so Christ's body broken on the cross provided for His new body, the church, which by His Spirit was "multiplied" into the whole world as the community of God's people.

So Jesus told His disciples, in effect: "It is for your good that I am going away. Now I am limited by My physical existence. But in going, I will send the Spirit. I will be with you now in a new dimension. Now *you* will be My physical

---

°Scripture quotations are from *The New International Version,* copyright © 1978 by The New York International Bible Society. Used by permission of Zondervan Publishing House.

body, spread throughout the earth, indwelt by My very Spirit. You will do the works I have done—and even greater, for through you My presence and My operation will be spread and multiplied to the whole world. You are My witnesses! You are now My body, empowered by the Holy Spirit."

So the church's evangelistic mandate is at once christological and pneumatological. Empowered by the Spirit, the church is to do the works of Christ. One detects no divorce here between the charismatic and ethical dimensions of mission! "For we are God's workmanship, created in Christ Jesus to do good works, which God prepared in advance for us to do" (Ephesians 2:10).

There are several implications here for the church's evangelistic mandate and lifestyle. For example:

(a) Because the church is called to carry on Christ's mission, its main concern is not mere numbers but with winning disciples and bringing disciples to Christlikeness. By the same token, the Church cannot be indifferent to numbers, for God is "not wanting anyone to perish, but everyone to come to repentance" (2 Pet. 3:9).

(b) Jesus demonstrated and stated clearly that His mission was to "preach good news to the poor" (Luke 4:18). He showed special concern and preference for the poor and oppressed. This fact immediately puts a biblical restriction on simply "going to our own kind" in evangelism, neglecting the poor, and using the "homogeneous unit" theory as the major factor in determining our evangelistic priorities. It warns us of the danger of simply going after those easiest to reach or most likely to respond.

(c) A third implication of the fact that we are called to participate in the mission of God is that mission covers all needs of all persons in all places. *The mission of God is the kingdom of God.* It is inevitably political, social, and economic, even though (and precisely because) it is fundamentally spiritual. Therefore evangelism includes witnessing to God's truth and justice in all areas of life and society.

W. Robert Smith was quoted as saying at the 1978 National Association of Evangelicals Convention, "Certainly we are to be compassionate of the world's needs, and yet, our responsibility is to proclaim the gospel of Jesus Christ."[9] But this statement already implies an unbiblical dichotomy. Showing compassion for the world's needs and proclaiming the gospel are not two different things. Every act of kindness and compassion and justice in the name of Jesus Christ *is* proclaiming His gospel, even though the gospel is not fully proclaimed until persons have been personally confronted with the truth claims of Jesus and their responsibility to accept or reject Him as their Lord.

In our evangelistic lifestyle, we need a holistic witness that gives both depth and credibility to our proclamation and evangelism.

2. *Evangelism is sharing life, and the church cannot share what it does not possess. Therefore a congregation's evangelistic fruitfulness will be in proportion to its spiritual vitality.*

A major problem with "Here's Life," and with any form of evangelism that relies heavily on the mass media, is that the gospel message becomes largely disembodied. The truth frequently becomes twice removed from reality. First, the gospel is separated from the context of demonstrated Christian community. This is already a step toward individualism, abstraction, and neglect of the human relational dimension in the reconciliation God gives. It already creates the danger of a serious misconception, namely that becoming a Christian is unrelated to the whole web of relationships in one's life. The medium directly implies that one can be joined to the Head without being joined to the body. This runs counter to Scriptures which say Christians have been born *into the family of God.*

In media evangelism the gospel is removed a second step from reality when it is presented either impersonally or in the pseudo-personal way of TV and radio. The prospective convert knows well enough that the TV evangelist does not really know him and his needs, so the words are hollow when the evangelist says, "I care about *you!*" Such professions of love and concern must often impress a needy, suffering person as being just as phony as such advertising slogans as "We do it all for you" or "You're the boss!" We all have a built-in discount factor for such propaganda, and we must reckon with this in evangelism. More importantly, we compromise the integrity of the gospel when we broadcast it wholesale *as though* we were in fact communicating directly and personally with individual persons in their real-life situations. There is a legitimate place for media evangelism, provided we recognize its limitations and use it in a strictly secondary and supportive way.

"Here's Life" did, of course, attempt to "personalize" the gospel message through direct contact with persons by telephone and at their doors. But in most cases such contact either did not spring directly from the community life of the local congregation or failed to communicate the community nature of the faith. "Finding it" undoubtedly was understood, in the vast majority of cases, to be a purely individual and personal decision, unrelated to becoming part of a distinct community of God's people.

My concern here is not merely that evangelism be personal or that it be integrated more directly with the local church. The more basic question is the authenticity and vitality of the local congregation itself. Many churches simply have nothing to share with unbelievers.

This is true even of doctrinally orthodox churches. We may argue that as long as it has the Bible and correct doctrine, a church has the gospel to share. But, in fact, gospel truths divorced from experience generally fail to communicate the intended message. The message may be *received*, but it is not *comprehended* as really being the gospel. Truth is not clothed in life, and therefore lacks the ring of authenticity.

A congregation must have more than correct doctrine; it must have spiritual life. It must be spiritually vital.

The practical implications of this argument are that the authenticity and vitality of the congregation are themselves matters of evangelistic priority, and that the gospel must be presented on the basis of personal relationships. The gospel is not primarily abstract truth but primarily personal relationships with God through Jesus Christ. This will be best comprehended when we present the gospel on the basis of personal relationships and through personal relationships.

3. *Spiritual life depends upon and is deepened by a vital experience of Christian community.* Genuine Christian community itself is evangelistic, and a church which is weak in community will be weak in evangelism—even though it may show "results."

Both Scripture and experience teach us the importance of Christian community for personal spiritual life and growth. Much of the dynamism of the early Christian church in Jerusalem was due to the fact that the believers "devoted themselves ... to the fellowship" (Acts 2:42), "were together" (Acts 2:44), and "broke bread in their homes and ate together" (Acts 2:46). They were discovering Christian community, and in the process discovering more fully the meaning of the reconciliation they had received from God.

Soon the Jewish believers were to learn a deeper lesson in community and reconciliation: Gentile believers were also to be fully part of the church. Later Paul called this reconciliation of Jews and Gentiles in one body (Ephesians 2—3) the "mystery" of the Gospel. Paul then went on to teach that God's plan is for the whole Christian community to grow together and grow up into Jesus Christ, the Head (Ephesians 4). Spiritual growth is described in terms of community, unity, and the mutuality of service and gifts.

This is why the New Testament does not say much about evangelism. It puts the emphasis on authentic Christian community—the reconciled life together that comes from being mutually joined to Christ and mutually growing up into Him. The implication is clear: If the church is genuinely a reconciled and reconciling community, the Lord will add daily to its number those who are being saved.

The point is that the church must *be* good news in order to *proclaim* good news. It *is* good news if in the congregation ordinary men and women are growing in their relationships with God and with each other; if in the church they are discovering new resources for everyday life, new direction and motivation for ministry, and deeper dimensions of what it means to share life and faith with Christian sisters and brothers.

I emphasize this point because most churches today are woefully weak at the point of genuine *koinonia*. We have allowed a superficial form of fellowship to substitute for the deep sharing that is so essential to an authentic experience of the church. In many churches, genuine community is such a lost dimension that few even perceive its lack.

Whenever real community has been lost in the church, renewal movements have sprung up which have majored on the neglected area. Historically this was true in monasticism,

Anabaptism, and other movements. Today the same thing is seen in the literally hundreds of new intentional communities which have sprung up within the past decades.[10] In style these range from the neo-Pentecostal to the neo-Anabaptist; from Christian urban communes to networks of suburban house fellowships; from communities with political agendas to those which focus primarily on the quality and depth of community itself; from those which are radically egalitarian to those which are highly structured and perhaps even hierarchical; from those living together in shared households to those maintaining more traditional living styles but committed to each other through some form of covenant. Over the past three years I have come into contact with a number of such communities, and have been impressed both with the diversity and the vitality of such groups. One thing they all have in common is the excitement of discovering the freedom and joy of intimately sharing lives together in common purpose and in allegiance to Jesus Christ.

Both for its own authenticity and for its evangelistic fruitfulness, the church must learn ways to recover the dynamic of genuine Christian community. Churches can learn this from contact with the new forms of community mentioned above and through studying what the Bible itself says about the community of God's people. They will discover, however, that the recovery of community is in part a structural problem. That is, real community will not develop in the church unless there are normative structures to nourish it.

As hinted above, I am not arguing that a church weak in community will be "unsuccessful" in evangelism. It may, in fact, see many people converted and added to the church rolls. But without genuine community there will be little discipleship. New converts will come to church and claim allegiance to Christ, but little will change in their lifestyles. Their patterns of use of time, money, and other resources will change very little. Their lives will present no real challenge to the built-in evils of oppression, prejudice, and exploitation in society. When community is weak, successful evangelism will do little more than hasten the church's accommodation to surrounding society. Evangelism without community and discipleship may simply speed the process of bringing the world into the church, rather than bringing the gospel to the world. This was true when the Roman population was nominally Christianized after Constantine and will always be true when evangelism is put ahead of the authenticity of the Christian fellowship itself.

We must learn that genuine community itself is good news! Community without Christ is not *the* good news, but *any* form of community is good news to one seeking a way out of loneliness and the depersonalization of technological society. This is the lesson of the People's Temple cult. It is the explanation of the interest and fascination today in all forms of community, communal living, sensitivity groups, false cults, and other forms of "groupness." People hunger for genuine community. At a deep level, we all yearn to be a part of a close-knit caring fellowship of people who know us well, and with whom we can truly share all aspects of life. This is true for the very fundamental reason that we are all created in the image of God.

As meaningful family life declines today, this need for community becomes increasingly crucial. So the church that neglects the understanding and experience of genuine Christian *koinonia* does so at its own peril. And it compromises its evangelistic witness as well.

By contrast, the congregation which demonstrates deep

caring and community increases the credibility of its evangelistic witness. When the onlooker can say, "Behold how they love one another!" he can more easily believe, "God is love."

The lifestyle implication here for the congregation is, again, fairly obvious. The congregation must give attention to building deep Christian *koinonia* not only for its own sake, but as part of its evangelistic strategy.

4. *Evangelism will be most effective when there is a healthy balance of worship, community, and witness in the local congregation. Therefore, worship itself is a priority for evangelistic effectiveness.*

I have already addressed community at some length. My emphasis here is that worship, witness, and community together form the balanced ecology of a congregation. The church must first of all be oriented toward God in worship. This is the fundamental purpose and priority of the church—to live "to the praise of his glory" (Ephesians 1:14). "To him be glory in the church and in Christ Jesus" (Ephesians 3:21). On this basis then the church is joined together mutually in the community of the body of Christ, and then turned toward the world in witness. Worship, community, and witness together make up the life of the balanced and growing church. Note the use of the terms *leitourgia* (worship), *koinonia* (fellowship), *marturia* (witness), and other related terms in the New Testament.

We do not always think of worship as an element of the evangelistic lifestyle of the congregation, but it may, in fact, be the most important aspect. If nothing happens in worship, not much will happen in the church's witness. It is clear that much of the dynamism of the charismatic renewal derives from the joy and power experienced by believers in the context of worship.

Much could be said here about the sacraments, the use of music and Scripture in worshiping God, the place of preaching, and other aspects of worship. At this point I merely want to call attention to the importance of worship and suggest that it is basic to the evangelistic lifestyle of the church.

This deserves further clarification. I am not advocating that the church plan a "dynamic" or "exciting" worship service so that people will feel good and visitors will want to come back and eventually join the church. This smacks too much of promotion and manipulation. I am pointing to the priority of worship in its own right, as the first purpose of the church itself. Worship is oriented first of all toward God, and worship must bring us to encounter God—who He is, what He demands, and what He offers; what the conditions of His covenant with us are. Worship is crucial for evangelism not primarily as a way of attracting nonbelievers to God (although genuine worship will do this), but because it is in worship that believers come to see the world from God's perspective and come to share the divine impulse for doing the works of Christ. It is this kind of worship that both impels believers outward in witness and, by God's Holy Spirit, empowers that witness to be effective in the world (Acts 1:8).

By and large, people in North America today have only the vaguest notion (if any) of who God really is. To most Americans He is either a cosmic Teddy Bear, an old-fashioned Grand Daddy, or an oblong blur. To many Christians God is decidedly less than "the High and Holy One who inhabits eternity" and the "God and Father of our Lord Jesus Christ." Our lack of real encounter with God in worship puts punch in the statement that if God were suddenly to vanish from the universe, in time even the church would suffer.

The church that is serious about participating in the mission of God and doing the works of Christ will take seriously the priority of worship. We can accomplish the work begun by Jesus only if we have the same consciousness of God's presence and reality that Jesus had.

5. *God gifts some people for evangelism and evangelistic leadership. Therefore effective evangelism depends on identifying, recognizing, and using these gifts.*

Here the basic text is, of course, Ephesians 4:11-13, "[God] . . . gave some to be apostles, some to be prophets, some to be evangelists, and some to be pastors and teachers, to prepare God's people for works of service, so that the body of Christ may be built up until we all reach unity in the faith and in the knowledge of the Son of God. . . ."

At first glance the role of evangelist here appears unclear or not directly related to bringing unbelievers to a knowledge of Jesus Christ. But note carefully what Paul is saying. First, it is in the harmonious functioning of *all* leadership gifts (apostle, prophet, evangelist, pastor, teacher) that God's people are prepared for ministry and the body of Christ reaches maturity. So the gift of evangelist functions in conjunction with other gifts. Second, evangelists are not merely those who win people to Christ. They are those who lead the people of God in evangelism. The evangelist is that person specially, charismatically gifted by God to bring others to a knowledge of Jesus Christ and to lead others in doing the same.

As this happens, God's people are equipped for ministry and the body of Christ is built up. Thus "the whole body, joined and held together by every supporting ligament, grows and builds itself up in love, as each part does its work" (Ephesians 4:16). Here is growth coming from the proper functioning of each member and each spiritual gift.

The church functions on a fundamentally different basis than does a religion or a secular organization. It is designed to function on the basis of spiritual gifts. The charismatic nature of the church is nothing more than an extension of the fact of salvation by grace alone to the areas of the church's ministry and witness.

So the evangelist is an equipper in two senses. First, he helps others become witnesses. Second, he helps build up the total body by contributing to its normal healthy functioning.

The congregation concerned to develop an evangelistic lifestyle will therefore give attention to the matter of spiritual gifts. It will be concerned to identify those with the gift of evangelism so that the evangelistic witness of the church can be extended. And it will be concerned with the exercise of other gifts as well, understanding that it is the proper functioning of all the gifts together which allows the church to become the growing, functioning body described in 1 Corinthians 12—14, Romans 12:6-8, and Ephesians 4:11-16.

How can the congregation round out this dimension of its evangelistic lifestyle? Here are some suggestions:

(a) The church should understand what the Bible teaches concerning the gifts of the Spirit. Therefore solid biblical teaching in this area is important. With this can be joined a study of the outreach of the church as recorded in the Book of Acts.

(b) Expect God to awaken various gifts in the congregation, and watch for these. Look for sparks of interest or initiative which may indicate spiritual gifts.

(c) Gifts grow out of the community life of the church. In the community gifts are awakened, discovered, and facilitated. Therefore the church needs to involve its members in various forms of small-group structures so that community can be fostered and spiritual gifts can spring forth.

(d) Those who appear to have evangelistic gifts should be encouraged and trained to use their gifts effectively. This training will include helping such persons to understand their gift; giving them training and experience in evangelism; and freeing them from other responsibilities so they can concentrate on the gift-ministry God has given them. (Peter Wagner suggests that in most congregations, about 10 percent of the members normally have the gift of evangelism.)[11]

(e) Since evangelism needs to be joined with nurture and discipleship, the congregation will be concerned also with developing gift ministries of teaching, exhortation, and other kinds that will help new converts to become growing disciples.

(f) The congregation should be alert to providing partial or full-time economic support for people with demonstrated gift ministries. We should rid ourselves of the automatic "pastor equals full-time salary" equation and rather think in terms of multiple charismatic ministries in the congregation. If the congregation employs anyone full-time or part-time, it should be those whose ministries have become so crucial to the life and witness of the congregation that the church decides to provide for the full-time exercise of these ministries. Such forms of service may be pastoral, evangelistic, missionary, social, or of other varieties, depending on the life and needs of the particular congregation. The point is that the church should put its resources behind the ministries which are most crucial to its life.

Through thus recognizing and facilitating the exercise of spiritual gifts, the alert congregation will discover widening possibilities of outreach and ministry.

6. *Conversion begins a lifelong process of spiritual growth, discipleship, and sanctification toward the restoration of the image of God in the believer. Therefore, evangelism must lead into this growth and the congregation should make provision to facilitate this growth.*

Biblically based evangelism does not focus exclusively on the death and resurrection of Jesus Christ. Rather, it sets these crucial events in the context of Jesus' earthly life and of His present reign. The fact that in Jesus "we have redemption through his blood, the forgiveness of sins" (Ephesians 1:7) is part of God's "economy [*oikonomia*] to bring all things in heaven and on earth together under one head, even Christ" (Ephesians 1:10). Or, as Paul says similarly in Colossians, God "has rescued us from the dominion of darkness and brought us into the kingdom [or reign] of the Son he loves, in whom we have redemption, the forgiveness of sins. . . . For God was pleased to have all his fullness dwell in him, and through him to reconcile to himself all things, whether things on earth or things in heaven, by making peace through his blood, shed on the cross" (Col. 1:13-14, 19-20).

In this Colossian passage, Paul continues that God wills "to present you holy in his sight, without blemish and free from accusation" (Col. 1:22). So he says, "We proclaim . . . [Christ], admonishing and teaching everyone with all wisdom, so that we may present everyone perfect in Christ" (Col. 1:28). As "in Christ all the fullness of the Deity lives in bodily form," so "you have been given fullness in Christ, who is the head over every power and authority" (Col. 2:9).

Focusing on Jesus' life and reign, as well as His death and resurrection, we see that God's concern is not only to rescue us from hell or redeem us for heaven. Rather, it is to recreate within us, and in the life of the congregation, "the fullness of Christ." It is to restore the image of God in our lives and in our relationships. Bringing all creation to harmony and order under the headship of Christ begins through bringing all believers to harmony and Christlikeness through the discipling and sanctifying work of the Spirit of Christ in the church.

The lifestyle implication for the congregation here is that evangelism is never an end only, but always a beginning. It is part of a continuing cycle of life and growth in the body of Christ.[12] Therefore the congregation must be as concerned with those processes and structures in the Body which bring spiritual growth and maturity as it is with the work of evangelism itself.

We see something of a three-step process here. Individual persons must be brought to the lordship of Christ, *so that* the church can grow up into Christ, experience His fullness, and acknowledge His reign, *so that* the whole creation can be freed from its bondage to decay and be set free in joyful subservience to the God of the universe. So we keep our eyes on the larger goal, and we join evangelism to the larger work of acknowledging Christ's lordship in every area of society and culture.

7. *A congregation's structure reflects the actual priorities of the church and its leadership. Therefore, if evangelism is a priority in the congregation, this will be reflected in church structure.*

A church's structure is a pretty clear indicator of what the congregation thinks is important. It is an illuminating exercise therefore to examine our structures—including official and unofficial patterns of operation and organization, leadership, budgets and financial policies, and church property and facilities.

We cannot guarantee vitality or renewal in a church by the way we structure. But we can very nearly guarantee that a church will have little life or witness because of the structures we build or allow to grow up.

Structures have both negative and positive aspects. Negatively, structures can grow up largely unnoticed which choke off the life and witness of a congregation. Positively, we can make those structural changes which will reflect the priorities we claim to hold.

On the negative side, we are faced with the effect of human fallenness on all our structures. Structure is always an adaptation to the space-time context in which we find ourselves. Just as architecture partakes of and reflects the culture of its period and place, so organizational and doctrinal structures are rooted in their historical-cultural setting. This is not necessarily bad; it is simply true, and can present a problem.

Structures become obsolete or restricting in time for at least two reasons. First, because of their cultural rootedness, they tend to be static while culture is dynamic. Second, all social structures, including churches, have a tendency toward subverting the very purposes they were intended to serve. These two factors are inextricably interrelated because human culture which forms the context for all political, social, and economic structures already is fallen and, at important points, demonic.

This whole problem can be reduced in seriousness, however, if we will pay attention to the *kind* of structures we create and the *fundamental models or images* on which structures are built.[13]

Here the difference between an institutional-organizational model or an organic-charismatic model of the church becomes important. If we understand the church primarily

as an institution, we will probably adopt (often uncon-
sciously) structural patterns which presuppose that the
church should operate like other institutions do—on the basis
of formal structures, hierarchy, delegated authority, and im-
personality. But if we see the church organically as a functioning body, our structures will tend to be more flexible, informal, person-oriented and useful for mission. I believe that
a basic source of confusion and frustration in the church today is that many give lip service to an organic-charismatic
understanding of the church while in fact our structures
presuppose an institutional-organizational understanding.

In summary, on the negative side of structure, the
primary need is to look carefully at structure to see whether
it is helping or hindering the life and witness of the congregation. Do our structures tend to impede and choke off
whatever life the congregation has? If so, some structural dis-
mantling is probably called for.

On the positive side, a congregation needs to ask whether
it has appropriate structures to carry out the witness it claims
to believe in. If structure reveals our priorities, we will have
appropriate structures within the congregation for the
aspects of ministry we consider important.

Although form should follow function, we do not
necessarily move closer to effective ministry just because we
create structures intended to extend our witness. Our ra-
tionale for putting up a worship center in a growing community may be that we hope to minister to that community.
But, in fact, the structure may become a barrier between us
and other people, and thus between us and ministry.[14] We
very easily get the structural cart before the ministry horse.
Witness and service spring from the effervescent life of the
Christian community. If the life is not there, our structures
will only extend or entomb our deadness.

But where ministry and outreach are already happening, we can extend that outreach by appropriate structures, conducive to the nature of the church as the community of God's people.

This happened in the New Testament church. Three examples are the pattern of home meetings referred to in Acts 2 and 5, the "Acts 6 Principle" of differentiating between different kinds of ministry based on priorities and recognized gifts, and the appointing of elders in local congregations. These were emerging patterns of ministry and life which were appropriate to the community life of the church, compatible with the culture of the day, and functional in the life of the church. Ministry was already beginning to happen; Christians were worshiping, witnessing, and serving. And as growth continued, appropriate structures were adopted with differing degrees of self-consciousness.

The implication here for the evangelistic lifestyle of the congregation is that the relevance of existing structures for the church's evangelistic witness needs to be examined. Do our structures propel us into ministry or insulate us from ministry? Financial, architectural, and organizational structures all should be examined with this question in mind.

An appropriate question here concerns the heavy involvement of most churches today in property and buildings. It seems to me this is a major blind spot in the life of the contemporary church, and a matter that seriously compromises the church's credibility, vitality, and witness.

With very little question about basic priorities, many churches move quickly into major commitments in real estate (which means vested interest in the status quo). In a society where church property is not taxed and where substantial financing is readily available, it is all too easy for a congregation to tie itself so heavily to property and buildings that its sense of mission and of being a pilgrim people is seriously compromised.

Consider this: A church of some 500 members decides it needs a larger worship facility. It is growing slowly, mainly by transfers from other churches. It features a dynamic pastor and excellent programming in many areas—although it has virtually no real outreach either in evangelism or in social witness and very little *koinonia*. But since it is seeing some growth and is financially prosperous, it decides it should build a new facility. The options of going to double worship services or starting a second congregation are not even considered. The congregation votes to launch into a multiphase building program with an eventual price tag of over $1 million.

My purpose here is not to throw stones at cathedrals, crystal or otherwise. It is simply to raise some questions about priorities. To emphasize my point, let us consider the following hypothetical situation:

A congregation of some 500 members becomes concerned about the problem of famine and spiritual darkness in many parts of the world and its own affluence in an age of poverty and hunger. What can be done? A committee is appointed to study the matter. After careful consideration, the committee proposes that the congregation launch a major fund drive, mortgage its property, and ask for cash and pledges in order to raise $1 million for famine relief, evangelism, and technical and agricultural assistance to increase food production in needy countries. What would happen? It is not hard to guess. The sanity of those advocating such a course would be seriously questioned. Go in debt by hundreds of thousands of dollars to take care of people halfway around the globe? Preposterous!

And yet, without blinking an eye or examining a priority,

the same congregation will tie up its resources and determine its focus for years to come by launching into a major building program with very dubious justification from the standpoint of genuine Christian witness. Such realities raise deep questions about the sense of mission and awareness of priorities of our congregations.

These questions are certainly matters of Christian lifestyle for the congregation. The church's fascination with buildings and property today, reminiscent of the Middle Ages, reflects the materialism and comfort-orientation of the majority of North American Christians. It testifies to the shallowness of our experience of community. And of course, when it comes to *church* buildings—which we often mistakenly call "God's house"—whatever critical faculties we have are further blunted by a sacralist mentality that says expensive church buildings are justified because they are dedicated to religious purposes. Surely God deserves the best! We forget that God dwells not in temples made with hands, but in the lives and relationships of the Christian community. It is the community of God's people that is the temple of God, not our fine structures of glass and concrete.

Again, my purpose is not to criticize buildings but to raise questions about structural priorities. What we do with buildings may merely be symptomatic of our attitude toward structure in general.

As the congregation comes alive to witness in the world, the question of appropriate structures for evangelism needs to be asked. Identifying and encouraging spiritual gifts for outreach will go far toward answering our structural questions and suggesting viable forms. The place to start is with provisions that will facilitate those gifted in outreach to carry out their ministries.

"Here's Life, America" was one major attempt to provide

an effective structure for evangelism. In that sense it was a good idea. The problem, as noted, was that it did not grow out of the community life of the local congregations. Further, it failed to zero in on identifying and utilizing spiritual gifts, it was not sufficiently based on communicating the gospel through personal relationships, and it was probably over-optimistic about what could be accomplished through the mass media. In short, the problem was an ecclesiological one, a misunderstanding of the church.

There is a place, however, for structures for evangelism. There is even a place for large-scale mass evangelistic efforts, provided these are conceived and carried out with integrity, are tied in functionally with the life of local congregations, and are not oversold. We need a healthy dose of modesty regarding just what can be accomplished through large-scale efforts, especially those which rely heavily on the mass media. And we need a clear perception of the dangers and superficialities of creating a mere "media church."

Conclusion

In closing, I would emphasize once again precisely what the church of Jesus Christ is—the community of God's people; the body of Christ; Jesus' disciples who continue His work; God's chosen agent of the kingdom of God in the world. How often we forget or compromise this fact, or fail to minister in harmony with the perception! Though it sounds trite, it still remains profoundly true that the evangelistic effectiveness of the congregation is based fundamentally on its genuinely being the living and growing community of the people of God.

5
How Churches Grow

CHESTER L. WENGER

I have no magic formulas to offer. I cannot even say this is how we have done it, but I have some observations, some convictions, and some visions to share. I hope that they can serve as an inspiration in thinking how churches grow.

Certainly we would agree that abundant church growth is desirable. A harvest that returns only its seed can hardly be considered a harvest. If one looks at Mennonite congregations in America, for example, many are not returning their seed much less producing a large harvest. If we are not winning our own children, how can we persuade others to become one with us in faith and practice? Fifty years ago my father observed that over half of the children of Mennonite parents left the Mennonite Church into which they were carried as babies. Is it any better today? One can thank God that many go on to serve Him in other churches, but many do not.

In 1 Corinthians 3:6 Paul says, "I planted, Apollos watered, but God gave the growth." We do not need much imagination to say that the one who plants is an evangelist

Chester L. Wenger of Salunga, Pennsylvania, is secretary of home ministries for the Eastern Mennonite Board of Missions. He served as a missionary in Ethiopia for many years.

and the one who waters is the teacher, but in the final analysis growth is the work of God. All else is of no avail unless the power of God is in it.

A few verses later in this same message, Paul changes the figure to that of a building. He refers to his work as laying a foundation upon which others are building. Then he cautions, "Let each man take care how he builds upon it. For no other foundation can any one lay than that which is laid, which is Jesus Christ" (vv. 10, 11). With the right foundation, it still makes a great difference what kind of materials are used in building. The building that Paul speaks of is the church which is "God's temple"—the place where God's Spirit dwells, and our concern is for a solid, durable, expanding construction. The warning to build carefully must be taken very seriously!

Many books and articles are published today that enable Christians to look at evangelism not only from a spiritual point of view but also from a sociological one. This information is advantageous because Christians can gain many helpful insights from psychology and the social sciences which deepen their understanding and assist them in serving the world. Truth wherever discovered is not counter to truth in Christ.

I dare to hope that the Mennonite Church is standing on the verge of a great surge of vitality and growth. And I think that the church growth discussions which are now stimulating our brotherhood have potential to bear much fruit. The wind of the Spirit that is bringing blessings of abundant growth to the churches overseas in Africa, Indonesia, and South America has also begun to sweep across North America. So let us prepare for growth blessing from God. Let us anticipate growth, and prepare for it. It will occur if we meet the conditions and look to God for the vitality.

We must turn our attention now more specifically to the question of how churches grow. I want to point out a number of characteristics of growing congregations and conditions for growth which I believe can be helpful to each of us. Many of these will not be new to you, but I hope a few will grip you and make a significant difference in your ministry.

Characteristics of Growing Congregations

1. A Caring Fellowship. Churches grow when the needs of all the members are being fulfilled. Each member must feel wanted and cared for. Special programs, and gimmicks will not bring people into Christian fellowship, but love will. What is needed is genuine love among the people of God not only for those already in the church but for those outside. As Jesus said, "By this shall all men know that ye are my disciples, if ye have love one to another" (John 13:35).

In this connection I think of the Bible Fellowship Church in New Haven, Connecticut, an inner-city black community begun eight years ago. I visit this congregation about once a year, and I sense a real spiritual community and a sense of belonging. The people seem to have found a new self-respect, new social relationships. The pastor takes the youth roller skating and on camping trips. Three choirs are organized in this small church—one for children, one for the youth, and one for the adults. On special occasions they have a common meal in which everybody shares. Many also share in the preparation of the meal. They give programs in other churches. One senses that they are a group of happy satisfied customers.

Last year this congregation baptized 20 new people and this year already 18 more have been baptized. This increase should bring the membership to about 78 persons. A church will not grow beyond its ability to care for its people.

2. Concern for the Nonchurched. Churches grow when they touch needs among the unsaved within their communities. The gospel is good news for every troubled condition of people. It promises *shalom*—wholeness, peace, and well-being. Some feel that the church growth, which many are talking about, does not give this aspect of ministry sufficient emphasis. We know, however, that caring for social and personal needs of our communities is an expression of the love of God. It opens the eyes of nonchurch members to the relevance of the church.

Mennonite Disaster Service, Voluntary Service, educational and housing ministries catch the eyes of people. It is little wonder that out of the Mennonite Disaster Service work in Elmira and Corning, New York, two new Mennonite congregations have sprung up in fertile soil. In Philadelphia currently the Diamond Street Mennonite Church is creating a center of ministry to the community which involves a Headstart Program, a youth activities project, and a community health center. As these programs are getting under way, they are experiencing a surge of enthusiasm in many who are not yet members of the congregation but whose hearts are turning with hope toward this body of believers. With an appropriate spiritual emphasis at the heart of this ministry, I have no doubt that within the next few years there will be a great swell of new members in that congregation.

One area of need which we have too often neglected is that of families which are broken or in the process of breaking under the tensions of today's society. What a challenge the church has to minister to the extreme pain of those torn by divorce. What healing and comfort we have for such with the gospel of Jesus Christ.

What I am calling for here is a task-oriented approach to evangelism. Too often our congregations do not catch the world's attention either with appreciation or with wrath because they are not relating to the needs of society. The early church stirred up both.

3. Enthusiastic Attitudes. Congregational growth depends much on the attitudes of the members. Are they warm and enthusiastic about their faith, their congregation, and their pastor? John Wesley said, "No man is successful without a strong touch of enthusiasm." Such feelings will surely spill over in expressed attitudes of appreciation for what is taking place.

The Apostle Paul underscored healthy attitudes and conversation in Philippians 4:8, "Finally, brethren, whatever is true, whatever is honorable, whatever is just, whatever is pure, whatever is lovely, whatever is gracious, if there is any excellence, if there is anything worthy of praise, think about these things." This verse follows his admonitions to "rejoice in the Lord always." Time and again when I get into a growing congregation I detect the radiant joy of a happy family. There is much singing, plenty of smiling, and a lot of encouragement is passed around.

A winning, positive attitude is basic. I do not mean a competitive attitude which downs another church! But we will not grow if we continue to see ourselves as a small misunderstood minority gathering on our own turf for a private time with God. As God's people we are to follow the One who goes forth "conquering and to conquer." There are many giants in the land, but our experience of victory in Christ will carry us through.

4. Strong, Stable Leadership. A strong pastor is a key factor in congregational growth. Strength of personality is different from authoritarianism. Real strength knows how to

deal constructively with conflict; how to preach the Word of God with power; how to lead in meaningful worship; how to be sensitive to personal needs; how to generate enthusiasm. Unfortunately strong people have all too often looked elsewhere rather than to leadership roles in the church for involvement in today's society. Reaction to the wrong kind of church leadership and authority has taken its toll among us.

I have noticed that in both black and Spanish cultures there is a great respect for strong pastoral leadership. People enjoy following a good leader. I believe that Anglo-German types will also respond to strong, enthusiastic, sensitive leadership. And I might add that team leadership will not avoid the necessity of real leadership.

It has been observed that churches with relatively long pastoral tenures grow more rapidly than those with short ones. My experience in Ethiopia also leads me to concur with this observation. Frequently when a missionary who was serving a young church as pastor was transferred or went on furlough after four or five years the congregation experienced a shock, and it took a new pastor a considerable time to rebuild.

Traditionally Mennonite congregations have had long pastoral terms. More recently we have been moving toward shorter tenure and a more mobile ministry. I believe a longer term of ministry can be a real strength if the leader focuses on evangelistic ministries and training new disciples.

5. Involvement of All the Gifts. A growing church requires the gifts of everyone. It seeks to engage all of its members in its life and ministry, and it mobilizes for this end. Too large a percentage of church members are merely spectators rather than happily involved members. A functioning, healthy body uses all its members. It has something

for all age-groups to do in the life of the local church.

One of the large Mennonite congregations in Lancaster County, Pennsylvania, which continues to experience growth has both a missions team and a church growth team. The church growth team specifically concentrates on the local community, and the missions team keeps the vision for missions before the congregation. And many of its members are involved in personal evangelism as well as worship and nurture activities.

6. Quality Worship. True spiritual worship is pivotal to the total ministry of the church. As noted in the introduction, the church is the temple in which God's Spirit dwells, and recognition of this fact is basic to all else. The pastor and worship leaders make a significant contribution to the evangelistic ministry of the congregation. Uplifting, moving worship services satisfy members in a way that fads and unstructured or unprepared activities will not.

We are talking about a vital and deep experience of the presence of God among us so that singing, Scripture reading, and prayer truly bring us into contact with the living God. People, especially new people, are not likely to return time and time again to a service unless they sense an awe and reverence for almighty God in the corporate life of the body. They must hear *His* word—His promises and commands—on how to live.

Growing churches are composed of people with high esteem for the Bible and who feel the call to minister its message to others. Healthy congregations have a clear identity with apostolic Christianity, not merely church tradition or cultural patterns. Teaching and preaching rooted in the Scriptures and related to life foster maturity in the congregation. Ignorance of biblical truths, thought patterns, and faith hinder growth.

Planning for Growth

Sometimes we speak derogatorily of "the power of positive thinking." Hopefulness, however, is a great characteristic of Christians. Thinking confidently and expectantly
of growth is important. For some of us this will take a whole
new orientation. We often focus on such things as church
administration, preaching, stewardship, counseling, or social
activities. All of these are good and necessary, but dreaming,
thinking, and planning for growth needs to absorb our wake-
ful minds as well.

Two important considerations deserve special attention in
beginning to plan for growth. The first is the need for
cultural flexibility. For example, Germanic Mennonites are a
cultural minority, but in their life together they usually act
as if they were a majority. Their style, programming, and
activities are all planned for one cultural group. Since, in
fact, many churches are in multicultural communities, we
need to cultivate flexibility and appreciation for other styles.
Missionaries who go overseas must learn foreign languages
and fit into the customs of the people they go to serve. This
is no less true in the United States. For example, the Steelton
Mennonite Church has five distinct cultural types within it.
The life of this congregation must therefore be radically different from one with a monocultural constituency.

How often we have been insensitive in small but important things. My wife, Sarah Jane, tells the story of how
she was offered tea in an Ethiopian home and refused it because she did not want the hostess to bother. One of her
Christian sisters kindly reminded her that this was a mistake.
She should have welcomed the hospitality rather than have
needlessly offended the hostess. There are a hundred ways
to cultivate this kind of flexibility and adaptability to the
groups among whom we live and work.

The second consideration is the *importance of friends* in communicating the gospel. The gospel is communicated best through one's friends and relatives. In such cases, the Word does not have to cross cultural barriers. Natural relationships and cultural ties already exist. It has been pointed out that from 60 to 90 percent of current church members have come because of the invitation of a concerned friend or relative. The invitation grows out of a desire to have others share in the meaningful experience of Christ rather than from the mere attempt to add 'numbers. The barometer whereby one can discover how this friendship evangelism is functioning in a given congregation is to note what happens with newlyweds from different congregations or denominations. Where do they make their church home if they have the option of choosing between her congregation and his?

As noted earlier, it is God who gives the growth, but there are things which we as "workers together with God" can do to prepare the soil and plant the seed. The following are again some suggestions which I hope you will find helpful.

1. Prayer. Closely related to planning for growth with anticipation is prayer. Individual praying as well as congregational praying for growth is bound to influence the direction and fruit of the congregational life. It was barren Rachel who cried out to her husband, Jacob, "Give me children or I die." God can speak to those who pray. When Isaiah was reverently involved in the worship of God, he heard the voice saying, "Whom shall I send? Who will go for us?" His answer, "Here am I; send me." Prayer is not only a great privilege but it opens one to the call for involvement in the mission of God. The chronic illness of a nongrowing church is lethargy, and the symptom is prayerlessness.

2. Evaluate and Plan Definite Objectives. Before the walls of Jericho fell, the Israelites at least knew that they had

an enemy, a battle, and marching orders. They had a goal, a leader, and a strategy. A church that is going somewhere must have specific goals and objectives just as an architect has a plan before constructing the building. People must count their assets, examine their weaknesses, analyze, evaluate, and then build upon their resources and strength.

Our congregations have some strengths. Strong community is one of them, but in this case our strength has also been our weakness. We have been too slow to include new members in our communities. When they come in, too often they find that our acceptance is more superficial than real. Has your congregation been able to absorb new members? Have you faced the problem? Have you forged a plan to solve the problem if you have one? Sometimes our programs of Sunday school, midweek prayer meetings or the quarterly missions meetings, winter Bible school, and even Sunday preaching are routinely continued year after year not because they are serving us well, but because they have become "sacred traditions." Has your congregation evaluated these lately to see whether they are productively serving the ends for which they were originally created?

3. Organize Active Small Groups. Today small groups are seen as an integral part of the larger congregation. Such groups may be Bible study groups, music groups, youth groups, service groups, fellowship groups, prayer groups, singles groups, or the like. People who are uninvolved in smaller fellowship groups often become inactive because the large congregation cannot meet their needs. In a recent meeting of the Eastern Mennonite Board of Missions, Richard Detweiler shared that the Souderton congregation has recently divided itself into twenty-four small groups all meeting at the same time on Sunday nights. He sees in this great potential, not only for congregational renewal, but for

the addition of new members. Each group is called upon to examine its function and goals and seek the good of each member. Here we need to emphasize again that the full potential of these small groups for the addition of new members to the church will not be realized unless there is conscious planning to reach out to others.

4. Visit Homes in the Neighborhood. We are inclined to react negatively to persistent callers at our doors such as salespeople, solicitors, and representatives of the cults. Apparently, however, the method is not totally ineffective. I read recently of a minister of a rapidly growing church who said that he visits a minimum of 100 homes each month.

In one of the fastest growing Mennonite churches that I know of the pastor has taken visitation very seriously. Somehow he manages to learn of every new family that moves into his community. Then he makes it a point, if possible, to be there when they arrive, and he invites them to visit his church. He also keeps a record of his visits to other homes in the community. He aims to get into every home sometime, but he avoids going down a given street knocking on every door consecutively. When a new family decides to check out his church, he makes sure to meet them and immediately assigns someone in the congregation for a friendly follow-up. Once new folks come, he says, his own people surround them and won't let them escape.

The gospel is made to be taken outside the church. Not only must people be invited to church, but the gospel needs to be shared in the home setting as well. Without some systematic way, there are many in our communities who will slip by without being confronted with the claims of Jesus Christ.

5. Plant New Fellowships. A growing church does not necessarily mean one that is getting larger and larger. A sign

of healthy growth is the multiplication of new fellowships. Growing churches look for places to plant new congregations. In fact congregations have been known to plant half a dozen other congregational units while at the same time they themselves have grown stronger.

Sometimes the planting is in the form of a swarm of bees whose leaving is a strategy to multiply. Sometimes it happens when a family or two is commissioned to move to a certain area and begin a work. Sometimes without public recognition members find an area of need and begin a ministry. Whatever the method, happy growing churches multiply their happiness when they become involved in planting a sister congregation. Like a strawberry plant sends out runners, the church, while bearing fruit at home, is involved in planting other churches for a greater harvest. Think growth and plant new congregations!

6. Train New Leaders. Training leaders is a continuous need and responsibility whether the church is growing or not. In our American churches we have not been growing rapidly, and still the cry is for good leadership prepared to minister to the needs of the congregation. We definitely need more emphasis on Spirit-led training. If such leadership is to lead to growth, we must put more emphasis on evangelism and ministering to new converts.

In 1973 we Mennonites began holding annual evangelism workshops in the Lancaster area. Our emphasis was on doing evangelism in a way that our congregations felt comfortable with. We are not comfortable as super salespeople and evangelists. I remember one workshop in particular in which we were reminded that our evangelistic work should avoid putting on a strange armor to fight Goliath. We were told that we should take the five smooth stones with which we were most familiar. We did not negate what others were doing with their methods, but it was emphasized that we should use our own strengths with diligence.

In these earlier workshops we discussed the characteristics of a congregation which distinguish it as a welcoming body for new people. We asked ourselves what kind of singing, worship, and Bible study would appeal to those with other backgrounds. Then in 1977 we began to reorient our workshops. We began to plan and to train leadership for growth. Instead of the annual evangelism workshop we planned a growth seminar to which congregations could send "church growth teams." These teams were not created to do all the evangelism of the congregation. Rather they were assigned to discover and affirm the evangelists in a congregation, to develop prayer partners for them, and to lay plans for increased community outreach.

Thus far we have had four of these seminars with sixty church groups participating. One big emphasis has been on how to absorb new members into a congregation. We have studied Art McPhee's book on *Friendship Evangelism* which was then later taught in many congregations as a Sunday school class. We have also studied James Kennedy's "Evangelism Explosion" methods.

In conclusion, I believe that the Lord is ready to do wonders among us. The age of miracles is not past. Where we look to Him for healing, signs and wonders will be manifest in our congregations. Physical healings and Spirit baptisms will be accompanied by a constant inflow of new believers into the body of Christ. I believe we are on the verge of seeing the church move into the evangelistic arena in a new way that will produce growth such as we have not seen before. If we allow the Spirit to fill us with His power, God will get glory to Himself by redeeming a people and setting them free from the bondage of Satan. The setting free will apply to those from Christian families but it will not stop there, it will include those from many backgrounds, tribes, tongues, and peoples among whom we live.

6
Evangelizing the Central City: Problems and Possibilities

VERN L. MILLER

During the last fifteen years a lot has been written and said about the inner city. However, for the most part, this barrage of words addresses itself to the deteriorated areas close to but not including the downtown business district. This area, called inner city, is usually the nearest mass residential section to downtown and may have experienced rent gouging, riots, poor maintenance, rent strikes, and all around deterioration. Such areas cry out for answers because urban renewal, which was government's answer to the problem, has not worked.

Cities, however, are made up of far more than downtown grandeur and inner-city blight which usually exist adjacent to each other. Many people have assumed that the central city and inner city are identical turfs, but this is not so. In most central cities 60 to 70 percent of the residential areas are stable, owner occupied one and two family homes whose residents are middle-class people, much like one finds

Vern L. Miller is pastor of the Lee Heights Community Church in Cleveland, Ohio. Active in evangelistic and social efforts, he has been a Mennonite minister in urban congregations for many years.

elsewhere. These areas, vast in their populations, offer tremendous hope for the future of our larger cities. (See the diagram, for example, of the geography of Cleveland.)

It is important to point out that a lot is already working well in this part of the city. Most of its people go to work or school every day and live comfortably in modernized homes. There are the usual complaints about high taxes and high retail prices, but there is very little evidence that anyone who is working is approaching bankruptcy. Although some exceptions exist, it is usually only the unemployed who run into serious financial problems.

Human services are adequate to good and there is general satisfaction with the return on tax dollars. In the middle-class residential districts police protection and sanitary services, street lighting and paving are good. The character of the schools varies from district to district, and their performance depends very heavily on the character of the neighborhood and the quality of homelife. Some schools are in trouble, but they tend to be the ones in or near the inner city. In the large city schools there are numerous special and accelerated programs not usually available in rural and small-town schools. These programs range all the way from individualized learning programs to specialized vocational education.

The city's greatest attraction is its many cultural, athletic, and entertainment opportunities, and many residents stay for that reason alone. People who enjoy variety, change, and the opportunity for continuing education are pleased with the exposure to cultural variety which the city affords. In this regard, one should also mention the rich variety of people with a diversity of national and cultural backgrounds. Cross-cultural communication can be experienced without leaving the state, much less the country!

The city is also convenient. While suburban and rural

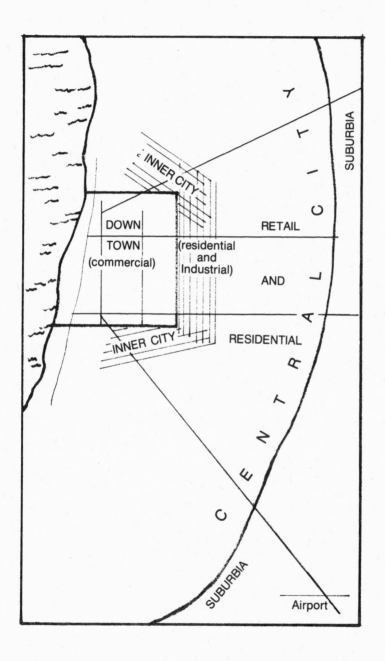

parents are taxiing their children, central city dwellers are able to walk to almost everything. And failing that, there are always busses and subways so that one can live conveniently without owning an automobile.

If foreign car parts or several bids on a job are needed, there is no problem getting them in the city. If a person likes to shop around, the range of buying options increases with the size of the city. So, if convenience is your pace, the city is your place!

The Imperative of the City

Throughout history cities have been the centers of civilization. In the ancient world they were thought of as places of security, and in Medieval Europe as areas of freedom for individual development. Recently, modern technology has changed the face of the city. For example, the automobile alone has played a large part in creating the problems of pollution, the breakdown in public transportation systems, and the flight to the suburbs. But we dare not abandon our cities because they are still the hubs of industry and commerce, and thus they draw millions of people into their environs.

As always the possibility of developing strong communities in the inner city and central city offers the greatest hope for the future of our cities. Urban communities house a polyglot of ethnic populations now learning to cooperate in order to achieve their common goals. The "melting pot" never melted, but the social mix has begun to demonstrate economic and social viability. Herein lies the challenge of the city to the church.

The church began in the city (Jerusalem). As it spread over the Roman Empire it moved from city to city—Antioch, Corinth, Ephesus, Rome. The Anabaptist movement first put down its roots in the cities of Central Europe. Only the intense persecution of these evangelistic Christians drove them into the hinterlands. Wherever they were even moderately tolerated, such as in Holland, Anabaptists remained in the cities. The traditional attitude of Mennonites in America toward life in the city is, in large part, a historical coincidence.

Theologically it is impossible for the church to defend aloofness from the city as biblical separation from the world. This position too conveniently insulates the members from being adulterated by outside contacts. Even though such insulation may protect weak Christians, and this is doubtful, it does not allow for spiritual growth and maturity. Further, it cuts off the possibility of effective witness. The Christian's protection is not insulation but the "whole armor of God."

The New Testament basis for church-world interaction is the command to share the good news with others. The Holy Spirit and His gifts are their equipment for the task. Evangelists, that is, those sharing the good news, must exercise their gifts fully aware that it is God working in them. "Woe is me if I preach not the gospel," was Paul's expression of a divine passion which controlled his life. Complete trust in God through Christ made his ministry effective as well as meaningful to himself.

It should be taken for granted that the church will take its rightful place among the other institutions working for the good of urban neighborhoods, and its greatest contribution will be toward achieving good communication and positive interaction among the various groups that make up a typical community. Without the spiritual component, society can only fragment further, and the conflict already so characteristic of many neighborhoods can be expected to escalate. We should be able to assume that the church will be composed of peacemakers whose presence and position will reduce tensions rather than contribute to them. This role will always be an overriding challenge to the urban churches. Let them become known as moral challengers of the status quo and peaceful advocates of positive change.

Problems in Church Building

As noted earlier, many of the local neighborhoods in the central city are racially or ethnically segregated—such as black, Polish, Irish and WASPish. This condition has presented a major challenge—and barrier—to the institutional churches.

There is nothing intrinsically wrong with ethnic neighborhoods which serve the purpose of keeping cultural uniqueness alive. The problem is that in many instances ethnic communities adjacent to each other assume adversary positions. In addition, when a neighborhood is in the process of change there may be confusion as to whether or not it is possible for several ethnic groups to occupy the same neighborhood.

In most instances a time lag develops between a movement of people in a neighborhood and the achievement and formation of its unique institutions. This lag is particularly true of the churches. In many instances the neighborhood is well along toward complete change racially before racially integrated churches and other community institutions appear.

Churches could ease social transition by arriving on the scene earlier and assuming a positive position on the matter of integration. In very few cases, however, has this been the goal of either the churches already in the community or the new churches being brought there. Most of these changing areas are served by segregated churches, many of which are also strictly sectarian. The contemporary congregation of the central city is usually the most exclusive social institution left in the community. This is part of the explanation for the almost total irrelevance of present-day churches to community goals. Besides negative social selectivity, present-day churches tend to be resistant to social progress and practical unity. They also tend to serve well, only their historical membership, with little or no impact on the unchurched or the other churches.

Some hold that the apparent aloofness of the church to the community is an image problem. That is, without a weekday teaching or service relationship the church *appears* to be unresponsive to the whole parish. Indeed if a church appears aloof it probably is only because it really *is!*

It is high time that churches whose beliefs have made integration possible act upon those beliefs and help to ease the way toward culturally pluralistic fellowships in changing neighborhoods. The church should not be the most segregated institution in the community, for this is a sad commentary on our social and spiritual backwardness.

Clearly this difficulty cannot be overcome without serious effort. We in the church need to familiarize ourselves with human relations concepts. We need to be schooled in what is required for good intergroup fellowship. We need to learn about other ethnic groups and religious traditions, and to share together with full acceptance of one another. We can and we must lead the way in this new period of urban social pluralism.

A second major problem to church building in the central city is the anti-urban prejudice which has been fanned by media coverage of riots and the decay of the inner city.

It is natural that we give only weak or nominal support to that which we distrust and fear while we enthusiastically support that which we believe in. Our distorted view of the possibilities for local congregations in the city affects our giving to them both in financial and personnel resources. Mass media and mass campaign evangelism receive generous support because they are perceived to be of God and hence trustworthy. No such trust or belief in the city congregations exists. Rather there is a spirit of defeat. My own city, the butt of numerous jokes in the media, has been referred to by churches as the graveyard of evangelicalism. Churches have fled Cleveland by the dozens to reemerge in the suburbs with strength, solvency, and rapid growth. So long as we view the city negatively we are in trouble.

Nevertheless, there are those who love the city and willingly accept the burden of not only its survival but also its success. Jesus wept over the city of Jerusalem, then marched triumphantly into it believing in the ultimate salvation of its occupants.

I believe that predominately rural churches, in particular, have an unconcious bias against living in the city which they pass on to their children. Scare headlines and media tendencies to overreport bizarre crimes have taken a sizable toll in negative impact. The publicity given the inner city in the post-riot period had largely obscured the existence of the middle city areas found in all cities.

A good illustration is the violence in Boston a few years back when the schools were desegregated. One got the impression that the whole city was in turmoil when the trouble was confined almost completely to two districts. Ninety percent of Boston was desegregated peacefully and with a spirit of cooperation. In our culture peace is not news and apparently doesn't sell newspapers.

We lived through the 1967 riots in Cleveland. The presence of the Ohio National Guard made it appear that there was a small war going on that was city wide. In fact the total area involved was less than thirty blocks. Although the riots were serious, the reaction to them was even worse. There were eighteen violent deaths, but these were all innocent bystanders shot by nervous guardsmen and police. Most of them were women and children. Most Clevelanders' lives were not affected except indirectly as we agonized with the victims.

It is crucially important for us to overcome these prejudices and to better understand both our real differences and commonalities in a constructive way. The epitome of worldliness is to think in terms of class, ethnic, or religious absolutes. To our dualistic categories of Catholic-Protestant, labor-management, black-white, rich-poor—and the list goes on ad nauseam—we simply add urban-rural. The U.S. and Canada, now more divided than ever, are being led down the dangerous path of separatism.

Although such labels seem normal and are often taken for granted, they hide the fact that we have so very much in common in each of these cases. Often we differ only in surface characteristics. Certainly we need not be adversaries. The accident of birth or residence or jobs does not put us on opposite sides! We are all people and many of us share a religious faith—if not Christian, then Jewish or Muslim. In any case, we are all people with varied wealth and diverse backgrounds which enrich our relationships. How much we need each other. How poor we are without another point of view. How unbalanced to only see the world from one perspective! When we see all of God's children as our full brothers and sisters, we will want to give and receive out of the richness of several traditions. The person who learns from only one source is impoverished. We need to experience and practice social acceptance across our ethnic and cultural differences. The church is the poorer for social exclusivism.

I might add parenthetically that the social exclusiveness of the church is usually the result of such exclusiveness in the family where those who marry outside accepted boundaries are punished by the restrained acceptance of an "outsider" into the family circle.

The city is an ideal place to practice the oneness we preach, to forget ethnic barriers and social prejudice as we view all strangers as potential brothers and sisters in Christ.

Advantages in the City for Church Building

The city, in fact, provides the church with a tremendous opportunity for effective witness to the gospel. The residential city, for all its problems, is a good and beautiful place to live. The central city provides the services enjoyed by a wide spectrum of citizens from suburbia and beyond as well as its own residents. Here are to be found clinics, hospitals, universities, research centers, concert halls, commercial and social services. Every day this part of the city is put to heavy use!

This condition, of course, creates disadvantages for its residents such as congestion and human pollution, but the beauty of nature is also close at hand. Shaded lawns, parks, and open spaces enhance its beauty. And nature can be as close as a backyard rose garden or a convenient park just down the block.

While the acres and acres of greenery and beaches that have been preserved afford natural beauty to the city, its real beauty is its people. They are like a flower garden with its variations of size and color and species. In a flower garden beauty is increased by its variety and the same is true in what has been called a "people garden."

Not only is this part of the city beautiful it is also right. It is right that a wide variety of diverse people can cooperate together toward common goals. It is right that its institutions include multi-racial populations who can forget their surface differences and concentrate on common goals. It is right that, for the most part, Jew and Gentile, Protestant and Catholic share of themselves without a competitive spirit.

The central city has a number of characteristics that can and are being turned into kingdom assets. The first of these is its social diversity which provides an excellent opportunity to demonstrate the real meaning of the gospel of reconciliation. Since most central cities have historically housed a polyglot of nationalities (beginning at pre-Pentecost Jerusalem), human interaction can be maximized! Some have identified the modern city as a microcosm of the real world. If we can make it together (black, Spanish, European, and Oriental; Catholic, Jew, and Gentile), perhaps there is hope for the nations to live in harmony.

A second characteristic is easy communication possibilities. The contrast between rural and urban communities in this regard is less pronounced today than earlier because of modern communication techniques and the automobile. However the city still enjoys an advantage. The urban way of life puts one in constant touch with people in a great variety of settings. Granted that these are often "secondary" relationships, but they afford an opportunity to communicate the gospel in one way or another. An act of caring or a word of encouragement when unexpected can open doors to friendship.

Third is the accessibility of people. Our modern cities are the result of large concentrations of laborers to operate the factories. Assembly line economies can be affected only where there are adequate sources of labor. This means that not only goods but people are accessible. Most everything is close at hand, and that which is not can be easily procurred. If a welder is needed, one is nearby. The same is true, for example, of an organist. No city church need go very long without the required staff—either paid or volunteer. All conceivable talents are represented by the thousands of persons at one's very doorstep. If staff is not available, the church is not doing something right. Either its recruitment methods are inadequate or its screening process is too strict.

A church like any volunteer organization must be attractive to the consumer. People will not become involved in an institution that appears exclusive or irrelevant. Of course, I'm not referring to a beautiful cathedral or building. The church is its service, style, what it stands for in the community, and above all, what its people are like. These attributes make up its composite character.

The central city offers a great opportunity for progress to all its institutions including the churches simply because both the market and the services are readily available in large numbers.

Planting an Integrated Church

In 1957 Helen and I moved to southeast Cleveland in a neighborhood referred to by most Clevelanders as the Lee Seville area. We moved there deliberately after much prayer and careful study, for our purpose was to "plant" an indigenous church. We had only recently been forced out of the ghetto by a new form of urban renewal called industrialization. This approach made refugees of over 5,000 displaced persons of whom we were just two.

There were several principles which we brought with us out of six years of inner-city struggle:

1. We would continue the low key, friendship evangelism

approach but concentrate on adult contacts first, rather than youth and children.

2. Our fellowship would be declared an inclusive fellowship, meaning that it would not only be multiracial but also interdenominational.

3. We would wait on the new community members for decision-making in order to maximize grass-roots ownership.

4. We would remain both evangelical and social gospel oriented in our approach to community witness and services.

Over the past twenty-two years these principles have served us well and the community has benefited immeasurably as a direct result. We also believe that God is pleased with the balanced mix of applied spiritual and moral principles with constructive human services. We have sought to minister to the whole person while permitting the members of our community to also minister to us. The result has moved us all toward being whole (healed) individuals with the necessary ego strengths for a united effort directed at the outgroup.

Recruitment Methods

We are a mixture of CHRIST-ians from every mainline and most not so mainline Protestant traditions with a sprinkling of Catholic Christians. (For a time, a Christian Jew was part of our fellowship until his death.) We called on over 200 families mostly on Saturdays and Sundays. We developed a mailing list of over 250 names and addresses each of whom received a weekly update on the developments of the new parish. We (the growing core of locals) adopted an inclusive name, controversial and definitive: "The Interracial Protestant Parish."

Soon our Wednesday night strategy sessions became the real heart of the operation. Out of it came a doctrinal state-

ment, a constitution, and a ten-point statement of community and parish goals. All of these were published in a
first anniversary edition of church and community news.

For two years we met on Sunday morning in the audito-
rium of the local school building. Each week we experienced
a gradual increase in participation. Curiosity and the desire
to be in on the ground floor began to take over. We
purchased two vacant lots at a very strategic location and
erected a permanent sign indicating our building intentions.
(There had been a permanent sign two blocks away direct-
ing people to the school where we met.) Of course, the first
sign stayed until we actually moved into our first unit which
was a 30 x 50 two-level building. Our services continued to
be a mixture of the better aspects of all our traditions.

Service and Evangelism

Soon after coming into our own building we encountered
yet another opportunity for community service. One of our
members proposed and eventually opened our first day-care
center. There has been preschool care provided for all but
two of the twenty years following that opening.

When the need for Hunger Centers in Cleveland became
apparent we had still another opportunity to serve an apparent need. In addition to both centers, which continue to
operate, numerous civic groups, including street clubs, use
the building. A nominal charge was begun two years ago
after two decades of free use. In some ways the Community
Church (as it is now called) is the most important address in
the neighborhood.

Although we never think of service to community persons
as bait for evangelism and deplore that approach, we are
aware of the enhanced image these services give to the
church. In service we seek to be inclusive.

While few if any worship with us because we serve them, many Christians prefer to worship where some of their resources are used in a visible, charitable ministry within their community. This is particularly true if the parish has obvious human needs.

Worship for an Inclusive Fellowship

Although a retooling of liturgical and ecclesiastical practices are only the surface changes required for an inclusive approach, the music a church uses tells the inquirer a lot about its inclusiveness or exclusiveness. For many years Gerald Hughes and his choir have contributed immeasurably to our worship with his solos and their anthems. From time to time we developed a youth choir that could sing the traditional spirituals as well as a variety of other soul music. Finally, under Laverne Rawls' direction, a permanent soul choir emerged which gives our music the balance needed for a pluralistic parish.

Preaching also reveals a great deal to the inquirer concerning inclusiveness. I have always tried to make it obvious that I thought segregated worship was ridiculous if not hypocritical. I realize that more often than not, I have scored sectarianism and the narrow ethnic outreach of most churches as contradictory to the Scriptures. I have constantly emphasized the social leveling and integrating aspects of the gospel as the supernatural outgrowth of a genuine new birth.

This emphasis is not lost on our audience. It is both our strength and our weakness. Some prefer to go elsewhere because they are not emotionally ready for ethnic or theological "mongrelization." But as the people become more tolerant, the Christian will become more interested in empirical brotherhood. This interest will lead to direct involvement and both blacks and whites, Catholics and Protestants will look for the inclusive church as their new frontier.

Acceptance and Assimilation

Most pastors and teachers limit their horizons to people who seem to be potential participants. Who are these potential persons and how well do we assimilate them? Unfortunately, we are attracted largely to our own kind and those who agree with us on the things we feel are important. Every church also needs cultural and personal differences. Balance demands a broader spread in traditions, backgrounds, and allegiances. Christians need the perspective which disgruntled and differing brothers and sisters can bring to the fellowship. Christian assimilation dare not be limited to the easy candidates who need almost no accommodation.

What are the rules for mixing with people who are different? They are as old as the Bible and as fresh as the latest human relations theory.

1. Consider every person a potential friend. Rule no one out even after several relational failures.

2. Become or take on the ethnic peculiarities of the target people. Eat their food. Digest their thoughts. Take their position.

3. Receive counsel more than you give it. Those who know-it-all may feed their own ego needs while driving the one seeking help farther away.

4. Suggest possible matching of new members' potential with kingdom goals as expressed in your fellowship. Offer them service opportunities and see that they are implemented.

5. Make sure the *acceptance is total* and not qualified or

limited. Show this by sincere socialization and identification without making prior demands on the other person.

Without assimilation there is little motivation for evangelism. Indeed, evangelism without genuine assimilation into the body of Christ is a disservice. Those who have responded to the evangelistic message and then feel rejected in the fellowship of the church are less open to the message the second time around. Not only must the church appear to be inclusive it must be skilled at mixing diverse people.

Conclusion

I welcome every opportunity to serve as an advocate for the city and the urban church. Sometimes I wonder whether the emphasis should be upon addressing myself to community programs or to evangelism and church growth. The latter seems self-serving, the former benevolent. Fortunately the two ministries dovetail beautifully. I am convinced that the church which best serves its community is a church that will grow!

We are employed by an institution which is judged not so much by how it serves its members as how it serves its non-members. The world watches and tends to see institutional integrity only in terms of whether or not there is a concern for all the people no matter who they may be. Of course, detractors shun the church for the same reason. Apparently, they believe the church should be socially self-serving and exclusive in its membership. When the urban church is perceived to be inclusive it attracts the greatest number of supporters. For this is the gospel fleshed out and fulfilling the unity of which Paul spoke so eloquently in Ephesians 4. People feel good being part of a meaningful ministry to those most in need of it.

7
Goals of Church Growth
HAROLD E. BAUMAN

The contemporary "church growth" movement begins with Donald McGavran, a third-generation Disciples of Christ missionary, who himself worked some thirty years in India. As a missionary he observed a great variation in the response patterns of the Indian people. In some areas people responded to the gospel in large groups while in other areas only scattered individuals came to Christ.

While still in India he collaborated with J. Waskom Pickett, a bishop in the Methodist Church, to do research on mass movements. This was published under the title *Christian Missions in Mid-India* in 1936 and reissued under a new title *Church Growth and Group Conversion* in 1962. This book might fairly be called the first of what has become a flood of church growth literature.

In 1954 McGavran returned to the United States to give the rest of his life to studying the missionary movement in order to try to determine what methods were actually effective in planting new churches. His first attempt at a systematic presentation of his views was published in 1955 in

Harold E. Bauman, of Goshen, Indiana, is a congregational consultant for the Mennonite Board of Congregational Ministries. He formerly pastored an Ohio congregation and was campus pastor at Goshen College.

Bridges of God. But his most definitive and comprehensive statement, which has in fact become a classic in the movement, is *Understanding Church Growth* published in 1970.

From 1955 to 1972 McGavran was largely concerned with applying his understandings to world missions and spreading church growth ideas. To accomplish this he founded the Institute of Church Growth in 1960 at Northwest Christian College in Eugene, Oregon. The Institute grew so rapidly that in 1965 it was moved to Fuller Theological Seminary and was called the School of World Mission and Institute for Church Growth.

More recently the Institute for American Church Growth has been founded in Pasadena, California. Leaders here are Win Arn and Peter Wagner, and they concentrate on the projection and evaluation of strategies for "growing churches" in America. The Institute is separate from the School of World Mission and Institute for Church Growth at Fuller but cooperates with it. These two centers represent the hub of the movement, but as it grows new local organizations are beginning to appear.

The term "church growth" was adopted by McGavran to indicate his special emphasis. At first he used traditional terms like "evangelism" and "mission" to convey his insights, but he increasingly felt he was not being heard. These words had come to mean everything good that the church does. So he adopted the phrase "church growth" as a way of talking about what he wanted to say. "Church growth" means all that is involved in bringing those without a personal relationship to Jesus Christ into fellowship with him and into responsible church membership.[1]

Basic Principles of Church Growth

Church Growth theology classifies itself as a unit of

missiology which in turn is a subdivision of the doctrine of the church. As such its central principle is that *God wills church growth*. Thus McGavran writes, "A chief and irreplaceable purpose of mission is church growth."[2] God initiates the mission, and desires all people to be saved. Thus Church Growth people talk about getting "a heart like God's heart," developing "church growth eyes," that is, seeing other people as God sees them—people who need to be redeemed.

Evangelism is conceived of as church growth, not only in the size of churches but also in the number of churches. McGavran states that the aim of evangelism is church planting, that is, establishing new congregations. So evangelism, seeking and saving sinners, means finding the lost children and *bringing them rejoicing into God's household*. Bringing lost people to the savior means more than winning individual souls. It also involves the grafting of wild olive branches into the divine tree.

Church Growth advocates talk about three kinds of growth. First is "biological growth," by which they mean that the children of members are converted and identify with the Christian faith. Then there is "transfer growth," or church members moving and taking their church membership to another congregation. Biological growth and transfer growth, they observe, will never win the world to Christ. The third kind of growth is "conversion growth," that is, the conversion of persons from nonchurch backgrounds. This is not to imply that biological growth does not involve conversion, but rather that an aggressive evangelism is necessary to fulfill God's mission.

A *second key idea* is the "homogeneous unit principle." McGavran defines the "homogeneous unit" as a "section of society in which all members have some characteristic in common."[3] Among the factors which may give the group a sense of homogeneity are geography, language, common history, and clan relationship. As a result of these factors the group feels a unique identity in contrast to the larger society. Social classes such as lower, middle, and upper economic classes, or ethnic groups like Scandinavians, Lutherans, the Balkan groups in Cleveland, and ethnic Mennonites illustrate the homogeneous unit.

The "principle" is that church growth takes place most rapidly within such units. People will convert to Christ most easily if they receive the message within their own social unit and are not required to break with it. This principle emerged from the McGavran and Pickett study of people movements. In the *Bridges of God* McGavran holds that churches grow most effectively through people movements rather than through individual accessions because in nearly all non-Western societies decisions are normally made within the clan or tribe rather than individually. Furthermore, each of these homogeneous units has its own pattern, its own rate of growth, and its own limitations for growth. Therefore, to do effective witnessing one must do sociological research and make use of the social sciences to determine the most fruitful evangelistic methods. We will note later how the church growth people make large use of the social sciences.

Leslie Newbigin, who also was for many years a missionary church leader in South India, comments on the way in which McGavran overturned the traditional evangelical way of looking at mission. He bypassed the "mission station," which Newbigin notes has been "the central element in the program of missions," and went directly to the people. Newbigin notes parenthetically that the phrase "mission station" is a contradiction since mission means going and station means standing still.

In the mission station approach the converts are detached from their natural communities and attached to foreigners and their culture. Two results follow. One is that the convert now in an alien culture is no longer in a position to influence non-Christian relatives and neighbors. Second, the energies of the mission are exhausted in nurturing the new converts to where they ought to be. Church growth stops and institutions such as schools, hospitals, and orphanages begin to multiply.[4]

One of McGavran's classical statements is, "Men [sic] like to become Christians without crossing racial, linguistic, or class barriers."[5] That is the heart of what he is saying in the homogeneous unit principle. We will evaluate it later.

A *third basic principle* grows out of the observation that in many traditional societies decision-making is a group process and not the decision of one lone individual against the group. McGavran thinks that we should take advantage of this process to press for what have sometimes been called group conversions. (It should be noted that in his later writings he refines his terminology. Instead of speaking of "group conversions" he changes to "multi-individual, multi-interdependent conversion, which," he adds, "is a very different thing."[6]

In his book *Bridges of God*, he explains this process. The group decision is not merely the sum of the individual decisions in the group. The leader makes sure that his followers will follow. The followers make sure they are not ahead of each other. The husbands consult with their wives. Sons pledge to their fathers. They ask the question frequently, "Will we as a group move ahead if so and so decides not to go along?" There is a group process in decision-making.

People become Christians, he holds, as a wave of decision for Christ sweeps through the group mind, involving many individual decisions but being far more than merely the sum of all the decisions added together. He says this may be called a chain reaction. Each decision sets off others and the sum total powerfully affects every individual. When conditions are right, not merely each subgroup, but the entire group may decide for Christ.

What McGavran seems to be saying is that where a close-knit social group receives the gospel and they have an opportunity to weigh it together rather than as individuals in isolation, a powerful interaction goes on that helps the group toward decision. Even though the group is helped toward decision by that dynamic, the vitality and the integrity of each individual decision still needs to be examined. Whether the group is the nuclear family, the extended family, or the social community which is involved, this principle is important for evangelism. We will refer to this again later in this chapter.

A *fourth basic principle* in the church growth movement is that the "evangelism readiness" of a group should be taken into account. Wagner writes about a "resistance-receptivity axis." At one end there is readiness for the gospel, at the other end there can be resistance. It is the flow back and forth between these poles that anyone in evangelism needs to be aware of. One needs to determine which segments of society are more open to the gospel.

The Church Growth advocates say that when a social segment gives evidence that it is closed to the gospel, one should staff that area of work lightly. But where there is a movement of people into the church, there all the resources which can be mustered should be rushed to take advantage of the Spirit's work. It is important in a time of rapid growth for churches to pay attention to internal strength.

A *fifth principle* of church growth is the recognition of the three dimensions of growth. One dimension is *quantity* or conversion growth that extends the church, the kingdom. The second kind of growth is *quality* growth, that is, internal and intensive growth, growth in grace and knowledge, building people in the faith. The third kind of growth is called *organic* growth by which is meant the emergence of other congregations, other congregations being planted.

McGavran insists that these three kinds of growth must be seen together as a unit. The ingathering, the nurturing, and the spawning of new congregations are all tied together. But, he says, there is a first among equals: the ingathering of new believers is first above the others. Planting the church is first. McGavran holds that as soon as we separate the concern for quality from the deepest passion of Christ, namely, His concern to seek and to save the lost, then it ceases to be Christian quality.

Do we understand what he is saying? He is saying that a congregation which is alive and winning people to Jesus Christ will have a different quality and a better concept of nurture than the congregation which is nurturing its own members but is not reaching new people. When the Lord's passion for bringing new people into the church is lost, nurture ceases to be Christian nurture. The ultimate goal to which God directs mission agencies or congregations is the effective multiplication of churches in the receptive societies of the earth. That is McGavran's directive.

The sixth principle of the church growth movement is that it is better to multiply congregations than to keep on increasing the membership of one congregation. Wagner holds that churches should actively reproduce themselves. This will be costly in terms of people, of time, of money, but the results and the fruit will be worth it many times over.

The seventh basic principle is one that is more controversial. Church Growth advocates distinguish between making disciples and "teaching them to observe all things." In short, discipling is evangelism, and post-baptismal nurture is "perfecting." Simply bringing people from their non-Christian background to confess Jesus as Lord and Savior and join the church is discipling. One should not confuse the "perfecting" with "making disciples." And further, top priority is to be given to this latter task. In McGavran's own words, "Thus today's paramount task, opportunity, and imperative in missions is to multiply churches in the increasing numbers of receptive peoples of the earth."[7]

Discipling, then, involves eliminating old loyalties and uniting people around Jesus Christ as the Head of His church. The tests of a people's authentic conversion are three: (1) their new self-identity as Christians—"our people are Christians," (2) their recognition of the Christian Scripture as the authoritative source of religious truth—"our book is the Bible," and (3) their house of worship is the church. The social organism is thus reoriented around Jesus Christ, and McGavran is convinced that when this has happened ethical changes will follow.

Once people have been brought into the church with a minimum of "social dislocation" the perfecting process should be begun. Perfecting brings about ethical change in the discipled group on an ever-increasing level of achievement so that a thoroughly Christian way of life emerges in the community. According to McGavran such post-baptism nurture includes activity like regular worship, Bible study for literates, memorization of Scripture for illiterates or semi-literates, leadership training, and where possible day-school education for Christian children. These functions, he maintains, are very important if a healthy church is to emerge.[8]

The problematic element here is the sharp separation and

distinction made between discipling and perfecting. Can we make such a separation between the spiritual and the ethical? Has the gospel been fully preached when love of Christ is unrelated to love of one's fellows? How, for example, can the gospel be preached without raising serious questions about such issues as caste and economic exploitation of the poor? And yet, one leading Church Growth advocate was willing to speculate that there was a Christian slave congregation at Rome with Paul's blessing.

As a Christian community emerges, it then has the task of discipling the succeeding generations ("biological growth"). In one place, John H. Yoder says that McGavran almost gives the impression that it is possible for a congregation to so evangelize its community that the only task left for the future is evangelizing its own children. That statement raises an interesting question in light of McGavran's strong contention that unless a congregation is bringing in people from the outside the quality of Christian nurture declines. I suspect that McGavran's hope that a congregation will so completely evangelize its community that thereafter no one with nonchurch background remains to be reached is a bit idealistic.

Finally, *the last principle* I want to mention is that the church grows by making large use of the social sciences. The Church Growth strategy holds that one should gather careful sociological data on any area being considered for evangelization. Tests should be made to determine whether the population is receptive or resistant to the gospel. McGavran undergirds this in his own mission philosophy by saying that mission boards should place 5 percent of their income into a Department of Research and Development. Five percent of their income ought to go into research if they are really serious about extending their mission work.

Implications for Congregations

What are the implications of the church growth principles for congregations in the believers' church tradition?

First, we need to be challenged by the Church Growth leaders' deep conviction that God wills the salvation of the lost. I am impressed with the deep and genuine conviction of the leaders about evangelism. They make it their life's vocation and passion. Their concern for the extension of the church of Christ shines through in an impressive way! They recognize the need for teaching believers to grow in grace, but this is never allowed to cut the time and dynamic for evangelism. The Holy Spirit has worked within them the conviction that this call is the will and commission of God. It is God's heartbeat and they are engaged in carrying it out.

Their example ought to lead us to confession and repentance; to see more clearly the mercies of the cross in our own salvation, and to experience more fully the empowering of the Holy Spirit in our lives until the conviction for evangelism is as strong as the conviction about any other area of our congregational life—no less. Such repentance will mean making specific plans to spend time in ways that evidence the conviction that God really wants lost people to be saved.

Second, we need to take seriously their emphasis on the church. It is the church's task to proclaim Jesus Christ as Lord and Savior and lead people into responsible church membership. We strongly affirm the Church Growth advocates' concern for a genuine encounter with Christ as Lord and Savior, whether in a group or individual context. We affirm their insistence that converts be lead into responsible church membership as part of the task, and not just the saving of disengaged and free floating souls who may join a church when they feel like it.

But at this point I say "yes" to our Church Growth friends with some qualifications. As I understand the New Testament it is the church's task to proclaim the kingdom of God, and that may have significant implications for how we understand the goal of church planting.

To proclaim Christ as Savior and Lord is to proclaim Jesus Christ who said, "The kingdom of God is at hand." He was and is the embodiment of the kingdom; and that kingdom extends further than the boundaries of the visible church. Orlando Costas in his book *The Church and Its Mission*, and Wilbert Shenk in Chapter 2 of this book vigorously insist that we proclaim Jesus Christ and His kingdom rather than the church. The church, they point out, is the result of our witness to Christ and the kingdom in the power of the Spirit. Thus the church is a product and not the message. The primary aim of evangelism is to preach Jesus Christ and call for response, not to plant churches.

Sometimes as I reflect on this issue I think we may be quibbling about words, and I do not want to pass judgment on our Church Growth friends by simply redefining words. But I think there are two solid issues here. The one is whether the mission task is based on the nature of the church or on the nature of the kingdom. If one says the kingdom and the church are coterminous, then the question is redundant, but if the church is not the full expression of the kingdom, then the question is very appropriate.

Perhaps it is more accurate to view the church as the "firstfruits" of the kingdom of God. The ultimate goal of our witness to Christ is the rule or kingdom of God throughout the universe. But a significant part of that witness is the new Christian fellowships or churches in which there is a manifestation of the new kingdom reality. This manifestation is a "first fruit" and not the perfect realization.

So one can say the goal is not to plant churches. The goal is to proclaim Jesus Christ and to call people to allegiance to Him and see the planting of churches as the fruit of that labor. Perhaps it is important to say this so that over a period of time we do not begin to think that planting congregations is the final end. Luke tells us in the Book of Acts that Paul proclaimed the kingdom and congregations were planted as a result.

A second issue concerns our conception of and language about the emergence of the kingdom as a reality among us. How shall we speak of the kingdom so that it is clear that we recognize God's initiative and authority in its establishment? To put it bluntly, building the kingdom is God's work. We witness to the kingdom joyfully proclaiming God's rule. We become instruments of the kingdom to demonstrate the new inbreak, recognizing both the now and the not yet. But we do not *build* the kingdom!

When Wilbert Shenk describes some of the signs which indicate that God's rule is present among us, he describes the characteristics of a new community—rejection of barriers that divide people (Ephesians 2:11-21), the experience of shalom, and the witness against evil powers.[9] That new community, called "the church of God" in the New Testament is not the result of human building but of the Spirit's confirmation of our witness to Christ. These are signs that God is building His kingdom.

A third implication of church growth principles for our congregations is that we seek the leading of the Spirit about where we sow the gospel. The Church Growth movement proposes two empirical principles as criteria for the Spirit's leading, namely, the homogeneous unit and receptive fields principles. But this poses some difficult questions for me. For example, let us take "receptive fields" as a sign of the

Spirit's moving. How are we to apply it? What is the biblical basis for it? In Acts 16:6-10 we have the account of Paul and his party endeavoring to go into two different fields and the Holy Spirit prevented them. Then the Spirit led them to Macedonia, to Philippi, where there was a fruitful field. I wish Luke would have been a little more social science oriented and had told us what the barriers were that prevented them from going.

Further, Paul speaks of crossing cultural barriers as being at the very heart of the gospel. It is not an illustration of the gospel; it is not an object lesson of the gospel; it is right at the heart of it in Ephesians 2:11 ff. The early church congregations were clearly composed of mixed classes and races on principle. So I have difficulty with the homogeneous principle as an indication of the Spirit's leading.

On the other hand, although we recognize the New Testament teaching to the contrary, we must be honest enough to say that we have not solved this dilemma either. Neither did the church of the first century. It is an obvious fact that before many decades the church became Gentile having lost its Jewish contingent. Furthermore, most of us worship in congregations that are largely homogeneous units. The attempts of the Mennonite Church, for example, to establish heterogeneous congregations in this country have been largely unsuccessful. I am sure, however, that people have worked at it very hard, and I sometimes wonder about the heartaches in St. Louis, Saginaw, and other places. So there are good reasons for humility on our part as we dialogue on this point with our Church Growth friends.

Newbigin's comments about Peter's experience with Cornelius put things in a light that I had not quite seen before. He notes that Peter saw himself as a very obedient Christian but in his vision on the housetop his self-image as an

obedient Christian was shattered.[10] How many times do we
see ourselves as obedient, faithful servants when in fact we
are not all put together and perfectly obedient?

A fourth implication is that evangelism follows the lines of
friendship and social relatedness. There is enough truth in
McGavran's observations about the process of group decision-making to make us pause and evaluate further. In our
Western individualism we tend to conclude that a decision
made for Christ in the face of family opposition is somehow
of higher order than one made with the family's support or
one made where all the family together decides for Christ.
In the New Testament, however, we do have households
coming to Christ, and the households of the New Testament
were not simply nuclear families—parents and children.
They were the nuclear family plus relatives, slaves, and
other close friends. Nor should we ignore the fact that
household decisions involved individual decisions as well.

Sometimes I think that we have read the words of Jesus
that one must "hate" father and mother in order to be His
disciple as a justification of rank individualism in decision-
making. In this connection I recently read an exposition of
the love of Jacob toward Leah and Rachel. The writer
explained that the Hebrew way of talking about a priority of
love is to talk about loving one and hating the other. So
Jacob did not hate Leah but loved Rachel more than Leah.
So when Christ says that one must hate father and mother to
follow Him, we have rightly interpreted it to mean that we
can still love our parents but we have to put Christ first. We
should not use this kind of passage to justify separate individual decision-making for Christ which excludes the family.

If this is correct, then should we not give more attention
to family evangelism rather than picking out an individual
from a family to evangelize? When we evangelize youth,

should we not give much more attention to the evangelization of the peer group if at all possible, rather than pitting the individual against the peer group? We need to learn much about evangelism that takes into account lines of friendship.

A fifth implication for congregations is that we should make practical plans for witness just as we do for other areas of church life. Church growth emphasis on numbers as a measure of our faithfulness in carrying out of the Great Commission tends to turn off many people. It smacks too much of the American preoccupation with success. It smacks of gimmicks to get people to church—a prize to the one who brings the most people, treats to children on the bus.

Just several days ago a flyer about a congregation where two brothers were ministers came across my desk. They were having a great attendance drive and the person who brought the most people over 50 got a free trip to the Holy Land. So when people begin to talk about numbers, and say that God wants the church to grow in numbers, we intuitively react against it.

But I feel we also may tend to react for one of several other reasons, perhaps becoming defensive. Discipleship is costly, we say, and therefore we need to expect small congregations. The way is narrow and there are few people who find it. These understandings contain biblical truths. Allen Howe quotes Marcus Barth as saying that there are two passages which show Paul's concern for evangelism, but his letters show far more concern about spiritual quality in the congregation. I could hardly believe this. Certainly Barth knows that Paul's pastoral concern for spiritual quality is the concern of an evangelist who traveled thousands of miles planting congregations, and near the end of his life wrote that he still wanted to go to Spain.

John H. Yoder says that to play the numbers game, either for or against, is not the issue. It is not an issue of quality as against quantity. The church ought to be a missionary community.[11] A nonmissionary community cannot be a faithful church. I fully agree. We need to humbly acknowledge the Great Commission in our own lives as congregations and begin to make practical plans to evangelize. We should set goals for ourselves that we can control. For example, to set a goal for 50 new members is a goal that we do not control. But to set a goal that 10 families will cultivate friendship with another family becomes an evidence of how much we really are involved in God's work of evangelism.

A sixth implication is that making disciples is a holistic process. We should evangelize people as whole persons. This implication actually derives by way of a negative criticism of the movement. One can appreciate McGavran's concern for discipling as evangelism, and still find his interpretation of Matthew 28:19-20 as leaving something to be desired. The problem is that he separates the main verb, "make disciples," from the second participle, "teaching." The first phrase is not the imperative "go," but a participle, "as you go." The imperative is in the main verb, "make disciples." This is followed by two participles that explain disciple-making. The first is "baptizing them," which includes the whole conversion, regeneration, incorporation experience; and then "teaching them," which is the nurture. McGavran uses the word "discipling" to talk exclusively about the first aspect.

The word "disciple" is used four ways in the literature these days. One is McGavran's use: to disciple is to evangelize. A second is Marlin Jeschke's use in which "discipling the brother" means mutual address.[12] The third, coming out of Pietism, designates the person's inner walk with God, walking in close relationship to God. And still a fourth is found in the writings of the Anabaptists and in Bonhoffer; discipleship means to follow Christ in costly commitment. Now, as long as we know what each means by the use of the word "disciple" then I think we can talk about it.

The more difficult question is, how do we "disciple" prospective believers? Church Growth advocates hold that one first calls for a general commitment to Christ; then after they are incorporated, baptized church members, their ethical nurture begins. In this, as John H. Yoder notes, McGavran is simply following the policy of most of the evangelical groups which he has served.[13] He differs only in calling for church membership as part of the initial commitment. The popular approach of evangelism today separates the confession of Christ as Lord and Savior and eventual church membership.

Newbigin asks, how can we defend a form of evangelism that says nothing about ethical views, putting them all into nurturing?[14] Is there a knowledge of God which is not at the same time doing the will of God? Can you know God without doing God's will? Can there be any preaching of the text of the gospel except in an explicit relation to the context of the world? Conversion is a change of direction which involves not only inner reorientation but also an outer reorientation. Newbigin rightly points out that the church in the mission setting does not dictate ethics but acknowledges the sovereignty of the Spirit who gives fresh insight into God's will. Each congregation needs to be related to others for dialogue, but decisions about the gospel must finally be made in one's own concrete situation.

I have been wrestling recently with the question whether a person can make a decision for Christ as Lord and not relate it to a given issue in his or her life. For some time I had been teaching that one can deal with the question of inner sinfulness as rebellion and willfulness without relating it to any particular issue except the question of mastery in one's life. Now I am no longer so sure. Perhaps it is precisely in the concrete issue that the inner nature of sin is revealed and must be dealt with. But we must still be careful to help people see that in surrendering on a given issue, whether it be in the personal or social realm, such concrete instances are symptoms of the inner rebellion and self-love that trouble each of us.

As we have seen, the Church Growth people say one can bring a whole group of people to Christ without talking about personal morality or larger societal issues. There is time enough to raise such issues after the church is planted. John H. Yoder comments that this is fine if when they are raised, the new converts are made to see these as issues that relate to the lordship of Christ, and if there is the freedom at that point for those who did not really want to become Christian to move out. The voluntary decision and commitment must be operative at that point as well.[15]

Yoder raises another question that I would also raise. If "converts" come into the church and then confront issues on which they are unwilling to make further commitments and move to the fringes, have they been psychologically immunized against the gospel? And if that happens for several generations, what will be the net effect of such evangelism?[16] And I would raise yet another, and I think, more important question, namely, what about church members who are facing a hard ethical decision and feel that they were psychologically manipulated at the point of entry by being deprived of knowledge about the real cost? We have Jesus' teaching about the importance of knowing the cost before we enter the kingdom.

On the other side, however, one can give illustrations of people who would have never entered the church if they had been required to give their position on such issues as war and nonresistance, but given time and loving nurture they became deeply committed on the issue. This raises the hard question of just what minimal teaching should be given to those who present themselves for membership.

One critic of the Church Growth Movement writing in the *Sword and Trumpet* thinks that it will have a very negative effect on the life and disciplines of believers' churches. He sees it as a threat in five distinct ways. One, it will encourage "the surrender of a simple biblicism and an uncomplicated interpretation" so that an "uncomplicated appeal to the straightforward words of Scripture" will no longer be possible. Two, the "hard sayings" of Jesus will be muted. Three, there will be a loss of regional uniformity in favor of congregational adaptations to local situations. Four, "rigorous [church] membership standards will be surrendered"; and five, "church discipline will break down."[17] My own judgment is that while the movement may contribute to these trends in some instances, it should not be blamed for them. Many other causitive forces are at work in the same direction.

What shall we say then about dealing with people as whole people? My suggestion is that our evangelistic method ought to be consistent with our understanding of the nature of the church. If the church is a community of belonging—a fellowship and close support group—then in our evangelism we ought to invite people into the group when they are ready to walk along with us in the belief that the Holy Spirit will confront them when the time is ready. That is, if we develop relations of friendship, whether at work or in the neighborhood, we should invite these people into our small groups, where we ought to be just as open and transparent as if they were not there. They can see how the alternative community operates. We ought to invite them into our congregations where they will hear teaching and testimony about the costly discipleship, areas of confronting the powers, nonresistance, and personal purity. Then when they do say, I want to identify with you, they have some in-dication of what they are identifying with. This means a change in our evangelistic method for most of our congrega-tions and for most of us.

In summary, the Church Growth Movement is brushing away our excuses for our nonevangelistic activity. It chal-lenges us to become effective, and offers us some under-standings that can help. But we should not follow uncritically. The choice is before us. We can become defen-sive and quarrel over their terms; or we can be challenged by the Holy Spirit, seek His anointing, and begin to give evangelism the priority it deserves in our congregations. Such a decision will mean practical planning and action.

Notes

Chapter 1

1. For example, Howard Snyder says, "The goal of evangelism . . . is the formation of the Christian community, the *koinonia* of the Holy Spirit . . . . The really ultimate goal of evangelism [is] . . . the glorification of God." *The Community of the King,* Downers Grove, Ill.: InterVarsity Press, 1977), p. 104.

2. In fact, a recent poll taken by the Princeton Religion Research Center and Gallup Organization shows clearly that the legacy of individualistic evangelical witness has been the devaluation of the church in the opinion of people who consider themselves Christian. Eight out of ten polled believed that one can be a good Christian and not attend church. Twenty-five percent of those who do not attend church claim to have been born again; and 38 percent, some of whom may overlap with the last figure, say they have made a commitment to Jesus Christ. See *The Unchurched American, 1978.*

3. See John R. W. Stott, *Christian Mission in the Modern World* (InterVarsity Press, 1975), and Ted W. Engstrom, *What in the World Is God Doing?* (Waco, Texas: Word Books, 1978).

4. Quoted by Alfred C. Krass, "What the Mainline Denominations are Doing in Evangelism," *Christian Century,* May 2, 1978, pp. 492-3.

5. See, for example, Paul L. Little, *How to Give Away Your Faith* (Downers Grove, Ill.: InterVarsity Press, 1966).

6. *Christian Century, op. cit.,* p. 492.

7. For other examples, see David Watson, *I Believe in Evangelism* (Grand Rapids: Eerdmans, 1976), and C. Norman Kraus, *The Community of the Spirit* (Grand Rapids: Eerdmans, 1974).

8. Stephen Neill, *A History of Christian Missions* (Grand Rapids: Eerdmans, 1965), p. 238.

9. See James Scherer, "Ecumenical Mandates for Mission," *Protestant Crosscurrents in Missions*, edited by Norman Horner (Nashville: Abingdon, 1968), pp. 31-34.

10. William Ernest Hocking, *Rethinking Missions: A Laymen's Inquiry After One Hundred Years* (New York: Harper Brothers, 1932) p. 77.

11. *Hocking*, p. 59.

12. *Hocking*, pp. 65 ff.

13. In 1978 a special commission of conservative evangelicals under the auspices of the Association of Evangelical Professors of Missions prepared a survey questionnaire which was answered by pastors, missionaries, professors, and administrators from both the evangelical and ecumenical traditions. Their surprised conclusion was that "on the simplest level, it [ecumenical answers to questions] may be an indicator that some of our evangelical prejudgments regarding the theological thinking within the DOM [Division of Overseas Ministries of the NCC] constituency need revision. Assuredly it warns us against the ease with which we evangelicals continue to judge books only by their covers. Does it indicate some theological shifting within DOM? ... From the same point of view, those outside explicitly EFMA/IFMA circles may need to do some radical rethinking about their mental caricatures." *Occasional Bulletin of Missionary Research*, April 1979, p. 57.

14. *Why Conservative Churches Are Growing* (New York: Harper & Row, 1972), p. 1.

15. "Measuring Church Growth," *Christian Century*, June 6-13, 1979, p. 636.

16. See Gallop material cited in note 2. There is no pagination, but the material is found under question 39a of the Gallup survey.

17. Reported in *Home Missions*, Home Mission Board of S.B.C., December 1977, and Edward Perry, *Learning to Fish in Upper New York*, available from the Upper New York Synod of the LCA, April 1975.

18. Kittle, *The Theological Dictionary of the New Testament*, Vol. II (Grand Rapids: Eerdmans, 1964), p. 720. I have taken the liberty to omit all biblical references and to translate some Greek words into English.

Chapter 2

1. James S. Dennis, *Christian Missions and Social Progress*, Vol. II (New York: Revell, 1899), p. 66.

2. Jonathan Chao, "Foundations of Indigenous Theological Education: The Beginnings of the China Graduate School of Theology,"

Missionary Mandate 4 (1974).

3. John V. Taylor, *The Growth of the Church in Buganda* (London: SCM, 1958), pp. 252 f.

4. Stephen Neill, *et al*, *The Concise Dictionary of Christian World Mission* (London: Lutterworth, 1970), p. 580.

Chapter 3

1. These two terms "evangelical" and "ecumenical" have come into use for the former fundamentalist and liberal for lack of better terms. Actually there is nothing to keep an evangelical from being ecumenical or vice versa.

2. The non-Western colored populations of the world were explicitly referred to as the "white man's burden" in the latter part of the nineteenth century.

3. I have known of missionaries who after many years on the field took the belated chance to study anthropology, and their shocked reaction was, "Why didn't someone tell me these things before?"

4. For a fuller discussion of this see my *The Authentic Witness* (Grand Rapids: Eerdmans, 1979), Chapter 2.

5. "Evangelism and the Gospel of Salvation," *International Review of Missions*, January 1974, p. 33.

6. "Report of Section II," *International Review of Missions*, April 1973, p. 199.

7. *Ibid.*, p. 216.

8. *Ibid.*, p. 199.

9. "... we are discussing the theme with reference to specific situations in which Christians have to live out their obedience .... Salvation *today* means always salvation *here*, in this place or that place." "Editorial," *International Review of Missions*, January 1972, p. 6.

10. "Salvation," *The Interpreter's Dictionary of the Bible*, IV (Nashville: Abingdon, 1962), p. 172.

11. Orlando Costas, "Evangelism and the Gospel of Salvation," *International Review of Missions*, January 1974, p. 31.

12. Alan Richardson (note 10, p. 181) has noted that in the New Testament all the metaphors of salvation are corporate in character; for example, he mentions "Israel of God," "the elect," "the body of Christ," "the communion of saints," "the fellowship of the Holy Spirit," "the messianic banquet," "the kingdom of God," "the church," "the new creation," and "the new humanity."

13. The use of the perfect tense in 2 Corinthians 5:17 indicates that the new has already begun and now is a continuing reality. See the NEB translation.

Chapter 4

1. Toby Druin, "Whence Cometh Our Strength?" *Home Missions*, November 1978, pp. 5-10.

2. James Engel, *Contemporary Christian Communications* (Nashville: Thomas Nelson Publishers, 1979), pp. 21-22. See also C. Peter Wagner, "Who Found It?" *Eternity*, September 1977, pp. 13-19.

3. Quoted in Druin article.

4. Win Arn, "A Church Growth Look at Here's Life, America," *Church Growth: America* 3:1, January/February, 1977, pp. 4-7, 9, 14-15, 27, 30.

5. George Peters, *Saturation Evangelism* (Grand Rapids: Zondervan, 1970), pp. 76-77; C. Peter Wagner, *Frontiers in Missionary Strategy* (Chicago: Moody, 1971), pp. 153-60.

6. See Howard A. Snyder, *The Community of the King* (Downers Grove, Ill.: InterVarsity Press, 1977), p. 177.

7. See, for example, C. René Padilla, "Evangelism and the World," in J. D. Douglas, ed., *Let the Earth Hear His Voice* (Minneapolis: World Wide Publications, 1975), pp. 116-146.

8. See Engel's analysis in *Contemporary Christian Communications*.

9. NAE *Profile*, 11:6, December 1978, p. 1.

10. See David Jackson, *Coming Together* (Minneapolis: Bethany Fellowship, 1978).

11. C. Peter Wagner, *Your Church Can Grow* (Glendale, Calif., Regal, 1976), pp. 75-77. This is a suggestive observation, but certainly not a prescription or limitation. The point is that at least *some* believers in each congregation may be expected to have the gift of evangelism.

12. See Snyder, *The Community of the King*, pp. 121ff.

13. See Kraus, *The Authentic Witness: Credibility and Authority* (Grand Rapids: Eerdmans, 1979), especially chapter V, "Hallmarks of Authentic Community," pp. 118ff.

14. The very architecture of any building we erect says to the surrounding community, "Some of you will feel welcome here. Others of you will not." Usually it is the poor we (unwittingly?) put off. On the other hand, there is no excuse for a shoddy or ugly building. We need structures combining simplicity, functionality, and beauty that say, "All are welcome; there is love and grace here!" But even more, we need to invite people to Christian community more than to "Christian" architecture. See my book, *The Problem of Wineskins*, (Downers Grove, Ill.: InterVarsity Press, 1975), pp. 69-79.

Chapter 7

1. C. Peter Wagner, *Your Church Can Grow* (Glendale, Calif.: Regal Books, 1976), p. 12.

2. Donald McGavran, *Understanding Church Growth* (Grand Rapids: Eerdmans, 1970), p. 32.

3. McGavran, p. 85.

4. Leslie Newbigin, *The Open Secret* (Grand Rapids: Eerdmans, 1978), p. 136.

5. McGavran, p. 198.

6. McGavran, pp. 302 f. As a result, Costas seems to take him to task for shifting his view. Since Costas does not give enough data to substantiate his criticism, I think it is best to withhold judgment. See *The Church and Its Mission: A Shattering Critique from the Third World.*

7. *Understanding Church Growth*, p. 63.

8. McGavran, pp. 325 ff.

9. See "Church Growth and God's Kingdom," *Mission Focus*, June 1979, p. 26.

10. Newbigin, pp. 65-66.

11. John H. Yoder in *The Challenge of Church Growth*, Wilbert Shenk, editor (Scottdale, Pa: Herald Press, 1973), p. 30.

12. Marlin Jeschke, *Discipling the Brother* (Scottdale, Pa.: Herald Press, 1972).

13. Yoder, p. 32.

14. Newbigin, pp. 151 f.

15. Yoder, pp. 34-35.

16. Yoder, p. 35.

17. Herman Reitz, "The Church Growth Movement," *Sword and Trumpet*, July 1978, p. 4.

C. Norman Kraus is on assignment in Japan and East Asia under Mennonite Board of Missions, Elkhart, Indiana. He has served on their overseas committee and on teaching missions to churches in India, Indonesia, the Philippines, and various East African countries.

Prior to his present assignment, Kraus was a professor of religion and director of the Center for Discipleship at Goshen College and book review editor of the *Mennonite Quarterly Review*. A student of both Anabaptism and Evangelicalism and its origins, he is the author of *Dispensationalism in America* (John Knox, 1958).

A native of Newport News, Virginia, Kraus earned graduate degrees from Princeton Theological Seminary (ThM) and Duke University (PhD). Aside from numerous articles, he is also the author of *The Healing Christ* (Herald Press, 1971), *The Community of the Spirit* (Eerdmans, 1974), *The Authentic Witness* (Eerdmans, 1979), and the editor of *Evangelicalism and Anabaptism* (Herald Press, 1979).

A Mennonite minister, Kraus is a member of the Assembly congregation at Goshen, Indiana. He is married to the former Ruth Smith and they are the parents of five grown children.